GENESIS MATTERS

GENESIS MATTERS

Michael L. Brunner

XULON PRESS

Xulon Press Elite
2301 Lucien Way #415
Maitland, FL 32751
407.339.4217
www.xulonpress.com

Unless otherwise indicated, Scripture quotations taken from the Holy Bible,
New International Version (NIV). Copyright © 1973, 1978, 1984, 2011 by
Biblica, Inc.™. Used by permission. All rights reserved.

Paperback ISBN-13: 978-1-66286-617-3
Ebook ISBN-13: 978-1-66286-618-0

TABLE OF CONTENTS

INTRODUCTION

You and I probably haven't met, so to begin with let me offer a little context. I am your average American male, standard model, residing in the Southwest, garden variety successful and trying to make something of myself with whatever time I have left. I was around 19 or 20 when my grandfather pulled me into his study (that's never good) and said this to me:

"Son, I have watched you for the last two decades, and this is the sum total of what I have seen. First, you are motivated by only two things: playing basketball and pursuing attractive women.

Second, you do neither one well enough to make a living at it. Therefore, if the Marine Corps is actually willing to give you a shot, I suggest you take it."

So, there you have it: high school, college, Marine Corps, business career. Married with four kids, all girls. (We couldn't buy a boy — I choose to blame their mother.) I have great health and a decent tennis game. I grill a mean steak, like cigars, and — at 63 — struggle now and then with whether it's time to buy the Harley and ride to South Dakota. (I might be too young yet; maybe when I'm 65.) I've had my share of good times, and some not-so-good times — some really good wins and some nice losses too.

But the pivotal moment of my journey came when I committed my life to God and became a born again, Bible believing, praise-the-Lord-and-pass-the-plate Christian. That was 35 years ago, and I'm still not over it. I'm just as addicted to God now as I was then, probably more so. I joined a church, got involved, and became a Bible teacher. Truly, God works miracles.

The reason for this book is that after 35 years of living with the Almighty, I feel I have something to say to other ordinary folks like me. Our God matters. His word — the Bible — matters. The buck stops there.

So, here's the deal: you give this book 30...no more than 60 days. If the light comes on, great. If not, rip it up and use it to light your grill. Bottom line, I want you to open yourself to the possibility that God is real, God is here, and He *matters*.

THE BEGINNING

In the beginning, God created the heavens and the earth. (Genesis 1:1)

So, there it is in black and white: "*In the beginning, God created the heavens and the earth.*" How you feel about this verse may well have more to do with your life view than anything else. Where did we come from? God. Just God. Nothing else. He started everything off. He's the creator of it all. *Everything.* Nothing's been left to chance. No random, unexplained mysteries here. In my book, it takes a whole lot more faith than what I have to buy the idea that existence as we know it just "happened." That makes for way more questions than answers. No, when it comes to who we are and how we got here, my bet is on a single, all-knowing, all-encompassing God who is responsible for everything and everyone.

So, for the sake of discussion, we know there are a couple of other theories that account for our existence. For starters, we have The Big Bang. You know the story: somehow enormous amounts of cosmic mass and energy have an intergalactic one-night stand, and PRESTO! The world is off to the races, so to speak. But with all due respect, then who made the mass and energy? Did they just *appear*? How did *they* get here — and what caused them to react when and how they did?

Then, there are those who suggest we all hail from the most basic forms of matter. I think the term used to take us *all* the way back to the beginning is "primordial ooze." (That's "Ooze," for short.) So, if *that's* where we ultimately came from, the question then becomes, *again...Who created the ooze?* Where did ooze originate? Who or what started the ooze oozing? And the answer can't be "the universe" or "the great mystery" or "the shining white light." Nope — too ambiguous, too speculative, too insubstantial. Give me something more concrete. Something infinite and all-powerful. Something like God.

There. I said it. GOD.

He is where the buck stops for me. No innuendo, no "bright lights," no mythology or astrology or reflexology or any other ology. Because if our destiny and our future are crafted by the stars — I'm a Virgo by the way...what's your sign? — then, once again, where did the stars come from?

So, there you have it. In the beginning...*God.*

THE CREATION

³ And God said, "Let there be light," and there was light.

⁶ And God said, "Let there be a vault between the waters to separate water from water."

⁹ And God said, "Let the water under the sky be gathered to one place, and let dry ground appear."

¹¹ Then God said, "Let the land produce vegetation:

¹⁴ And God said, "Let there be lights in the vault of the sky to separate the day from the night,

²⁰ And God said, "Let the water teem with living creatures, and let birds fly above the earth across the vault of the sky."

²⁴ And God said, "Let the land produce living creatures according to their kinds:

²⁶ Then God said, "Let us make mankind in our image, in our likeness, so that they may rule over the fish in the sea and the birds in the sky, over the livestock and all the wild animals,[a] and over all the creatures that move along the ground."

[31] God saw all that he had made, and it was very good.

2:2 By the seventh day. God had finished the work he had been doing. (Genesis 1:3 - 2:2)

That's one whale of a week.

I am no astronomer, scientist, physicist, engineer, or archeologist, but I *am* a pragmatic guy, and what I'm seeing here is an order to how things were made. There is structure. You wouldn't make man and woman first, or third, or fifth... you'd make them *after* the rest of the infrastructure was built. If you create life, you have to have the environment in place to sustain it. And there's no way that happens by chance — just no way.

Let me suggest one more point of significance. Huge significance. When God made the first man (Adam) and woman (Eve), He described them in a way that was unique to them. Specifically, God said that He made them "in His own image." No planet, no solar system, no plant, animal, or anything else in the universe was assigned that descriptor — it was reserved just for them. And as it was for Adam and Eve, so it is for you and me. We have the special distinction of being made in God's own image. So, if you want to get a glimpse of what God may be like in some way, look no further — it's us! (Or at least it's *supposed* to be.) We are created to be the movie trailer of what God Himself is like; we are the preview, the image of Him.

Wear that proudly. Don't take it for granted. You may be at a place where your self-esteem is lower than low, and you don't feel that you're an image of anything good. I respect that, but this God-given descriptor isn't based on what you or I think, but on what God *says*. It's not about how we feel, it's about who we *are* — and we had nothing to do with it. It's how we're made.

And here's one last thing to note: The mention of God resting on the seventh day.[1] If God Almighty saw fit to institute a policy of rest after *His* labor, then that probably means it's a good plan for us too. I'll take it — there is just something that feels really good about that. So, while you are out there making your mark and climbing the ladder, take a rest yourself. You'll feel better, live longer, and probably be more pleasant to be around.

---

[1] Genesis 2:3

THERE'S JUST ONE THING

¹⁵ The Lord God took the man and put him in the Garden of Eden to work it and take care of it. ¹⁶ And the L<small>ORD</small> God commanded the man, "You are free to eat from any tree in the garden; ¹⁷ but you must not eat from the tree of the knowledge of good and evil, for when you eat from it you will certainly die."

¹⁸ The L<small>ORD</small> God said, "It is not good for the man to be alone. I will make a helper suitable for him." (Genesis 2:15-18)

I wonder if you have some basic thought or idea of what the rules of the sandbox might have been when God put the first people on the earth? Specifically, do you know what God said about the code of conduct for us while we are here? I imagine at least some of you would think of the Ten Commandments at a minimum, or perhaps the Golden Rule. But for the record, just to be *very* clear, when all this started with one man and one woman in the resort destination known as the Garden of Eden (which, by the way, should *not* be confused with The Garden of Eden in Lucas, Kansas — pop. 393), there *were* no Ten Commandments, no regulations, no by-laws, deed restrictions or zoning ordinances, no small print disclaimers, protocols, or standards.

For all intents and purposes, what Adam and Eve *really* had from day one was freedom — lots and lots and lots of it. Their

existence was just as perfect and pure as it could be. No aster-
isks, no sidebars, no addendums — nothing hidden in the weeds
— just straight up, home-grown, gorgeous, grass-fed, unadulter-
ated *freedom*! I mean, just live life to its fullest, enjoy God's great
green earth to the max, revel in the creation of things and enjoy!
Think the scenery in La Jolla, the mountains of Montana, or even
the wide, flat prairies of Lubbock (What can I say ? Have a kid at
Texas Tech) -- open, unspoiled, and ready to be explored. *That* was
how it was supposed to be — all good, all the time, all for them.

Before we go on, we need to get something straight here —
really straight. If you've grown up hearing or thinking that life
is one big monster pain, and it isn't a matter of whether you'll
be miserable, only of *when* and *how* you'll be miserable...that
somehow God doesn't know, doesn't care, or isn't interested in
your experience while you're here — with all due respect, you
have it *all* wrong. Before you find yourself neck deep in some
really bad theology, let me set the record straight. You really, *really*
need to get this part right. Are you ready? Here it is:

GOD MEANT LIFE TO BE GOOD.

You understand me? One more time:

GOD MEANT LIFE TO BE GOOD.

That is the deal. That is what I am in it for. That is where it's
at. If you believe that religion and being right with the Almighty
is all about rules and regs, do's and don'ts, guilt and shame, you
can't do this, you can't do that, keeping score, and on and on and
on...oh man, you've missed it. You've missed it *bad*. If someone's
told you otherwise, have them call me ASAP.

When God put all the time and trouble into making life all that
we know it to be, please understand that everything, *everything*,

was done for one ultimate purpose: to give us a magnificent venue to dwell in and enjoy while we are in right relationship with Him! That's it! Don't make this hard! Don't blow this! And don't throw the book down just yet. I'll get to the pain part in a minute — but for now, I want you to get your head wrapped around the fact that when this all started, God's agenda was simple: HE MEANT LIFE TO BE GOOD.

So, with that in mind, there's one very important item that needs our attention. For our first couple, Adam and Eve, God gave just one rule. One admonition if you will. One "don't" in a whole wide world of "do's." In a world that was meant to be a great big divine *yes*, there was just one single, solitary, simple no: Just don't eat the fruit from that *one* tree. That's it. Nothing more to it. Just no eating fruit from one tree of many...and there were plenty of trees with really good fruit. Stay away from the forbidden tree. *That* tree. Eat whatever you want from all the other trees, just steer clear of that one. Not good for you man — it will mess you up. Not worth it sister — just stay away. This is not hard sweetheart...not hard at all.

Just leave one single tree alone, and we're *good*.

THE BOMBSHELL

Now the serpent was more crafty than any of the wild animals the Lord *God had made. He said to the woman, "Did God really say, 'You must not eat from any tree in the garden'?"*

² The woman said to the serpent, "We may eat fruit from the trees in the garden, ³ but God did say, 'You must not eat fruit from the tree that is in the middle of the garden, and you must not touch it, or you will die.'"

⁴ "You will not certainly die," the serpent said to the woman. ⁵ "For God knows that when you eat from it your eyes will be opened, and you will be like God, knowing good and evil."

⁶ When the woman saw that the fruit of the tree was good for food and pleasing to the eye, and also desirable for gaining wisdom, she took some and ate it. She also gave some to her husband, who was with her, and he ate it. ⁷ Then the eyes of both of them were opened, and they realized they were naked; so they sewed fig leaves together and made coverings for themselves. (Genesis 3:1-7)

S o, we have paradise. We have everything right, everything tight. No stress, no strain, no worry, no guilt, no hurt, no pain, no anger, no sickness...does it get any better? Truly and literally, it's heaven on earth. How could they possibly mess *that* up?

But you know they did.

Of course they did.

Just one rule. One warning. One tiny ask, man — one single, simple admonition: don't eat *that* fruit from *that* tree. Could it be any simpler?

So, of course, the question for the ages is, *why*? Why would they do this? Let's be clear, you rewind this and put me in a place surrounded by beauty, abundance, and prosperity; a place where every day is a good day, and where I can enjoy God and His great green Earth every moment, grow great food, take care of the place, populate the earth with my wife, go to bed, get up and do it again the next day, etc., etc. ... and all I have to do to keep the wheels on is to KEEP AWAY FROM ONE STUPID TREE? You know, I have done some really dumb things in my life, but I've GOT to believe that I wouldn't have been so unbelievably ignorant as to blow all that up...I just can't see it.

But you know, what our original ancestors were guilty of that infamous day is something that you and I deal with as well. It is that tendency, that desire, that longing that's in all of us to make it "all about me." It's what *we* want, when we want it. It's about advancing our agenda, and ultimately, doing what we think will make us happy. We call the shots, we know what's best, and regardless of what might be better or right, if the instruction we receive doesn't line up with what we *feel*...well then, everything is up for grabs. It's open season on obedience.

So, here's what you have to know: when God made Paradise — life at its finest — another element was in play. It was the expectation that man and woman would live in this environment and have a right relationship with God every step of the way. Let's stop here for a moment because this is big. Really big. Maybe the biggest thing you get out of this book. You always hear how important it is to have a purpose for living, right? And how equally important it is to have goals, dreams, and aspirations. Some suggest that having that purpose and those goals will bring true and real fulfillment. So let me help you with that. After it's all said and done, I *know* what the major purpose and goal is for all of us. It's the same for everyone. It doesn't matter who you are, where you come from, what you've got or where you're going. The primary driver for our lives is this:

WE ARE TO BE RIGHTLY RELATED TO GOD.

That is why we're here and what we are about: WE ARE TO BE RIGHTLY RELATED TO GOD. That's it. Just stick a fork right in the middle of it. We get this one right, and the rest of it flows downhill. You see, when God put the earth together for His enjoyment and ours, part of that enjoyment was that we would have, *must* have, a right relationship with God, and then right relations with one another. The big secret is, whatever it is you want, whatever it is that you think you're missing, whatever it is that you think will fill the holes and gaps in your little life and mine — being in right relationship with God is what will get it right. Every time. You are not an exception, and neither am I. If we all really believed that, the Problem Index that we experience personally and collectively would go *seriously* down.

That apple represents choice. As it was for Adam and Eve, so it is for you and me. We want what is best for ourselves — we want to maximize our experience on this side of heaven. And *God wants that too*, but our way may not line up with his way. When it doesn't, we can rationalize: A "right relationship with God" is nice and it preaches well, but c'mon baby, we're in the real world out here — *we* know what's best! I mean, if it feels, looks, smells, tastes, sounds, and seems good, then just do it!

You and I *always* have a choice to make — is it our way, or God's way? The "knock" on God is that he is not about our joy, our peace, or our fulfillment...that He's about something else: denial of self, abstinence, tough love, discipline, judgment, punishment, whatever. That's where a lot of us are, and to be really blunt, we just miss it. You and I have to realize that God is for us, God is with us, God is wanting the best for us, and further, he has a roadmap for us to experience all of it. But there will always be those apples that give us the illusion that we know how to get the best that life has to offer, but God's not in it, I don't want it! I may *think* I want it, or I may really desire it, but again, if God isn't in it, if it doesn't line up with what He has to say, then I will pass.

I've learned that if I have to say "no" to one thing, it's only because I know there is a bigger "yes" somewhere else. You must believe that. If Adam and Eve had said "no" to eating that apple way back when, a whole lot more "yeses" would have been there, but I digress. Suffice it to say, whatever happens or doesn't happen to me from here on out, I know that I don't want to eat any more of those freaking deadly apples that come my way. They always look great, but I don't want any more to do with them. It's just not worth it.

THE FALLOUT

23 therefore the LORD God sent him out of the Garden of Eden, to cultivate the ground from which he was taken. 24 So He drove the man out; and at the east of the Garden of Eden He stationed the cherubim and the flaming sword which turned every direction to guard the way to the tree of life. (Genesis 3:23-24)

I try to think about how to put some lipstick on this, but it pretty much is what it is. Once sin (that's the eating of the apple) made its entrance, changes were made. Namely, Paradise City and sin don't mix. Doing things God's way and *not* doing things God's way won't jell — it just doesn't work. The perfect plan, the perfect life, leaves no room for sin. Perfection can't have an asterisk next to it. Close is for horseshoes. There is no "pretty good" clause in God's instruction. Perfection is perfection, and anything less has to go. So, Adam and Eve have to go.

Sounds tough, not fair, a little harsh, but that's the way it is.

So instead of labeling some things right and some things wrong, we'd rather throw everything in a bowl, mix it together, and call it all *relative*. You know, right and wrong is what we make it to be, certainly not what God says it is. *We* determine right and wrong, thank you very much, and by damn, nobody, *nobody*, from The Almighty on down will tell us otherwise! But bottom line, there were real consequences for Adam and Eve in not doing what God told them to do and not do. Like it or not, that's just the way it was.

It's In The Blood

Now the man had relations with his wife Eve, and she conceived and gave birth to Cain, and she said, "I have obtained a male child with the help of the LORD." *² And again, she gave birth to his brother Abel. Now Abel was a keeper of flocks, but Cain was a cultivator of the ground. ³ So it came about in the course of time that Cain brought an offering to the LORD from the fruit of the ground. ⁴ Abel, on his part also brought an offering, from the firstborn of his flock and from their fat portions. And the LORD had regard for Abel and his offering; ⁵ but for Cain and his offering He had no regard. So Cain became very angry and his face was gloomy. ⁶ Then the LORD said to Cain, "Why are you angry? And why is your face gloomy? ⁷ If you do well, will your face not be cheerful? And if you do not do well, sin is lurking at the door; and its desire is for you, but you must master it." ⁸ Cain talked to his brother Abel; and it happened that when they were in the field Cain rose up against his brother Abel and killed him. (Genesis 4: 1-8)*

The story goes on, but our favorite couple are no longer in the Garden. They've been banished "east of Eden." They now live in an imperfect world, and they are imperfect people. But as time passes, they stay together, move forward, and have a family.

They have two sons, one named Cain, the other, Abel. We don't know much about them, but what we *do* know is that Cain was resentful of his brother. That's not the half of it. How about angry? As in angry enough to kill his baby brother over offerings given to the Lord? Abel made an offering that pleased God, Cain didn't, and God let that be known. Resentment, jealousy, and outrage led Cain to kill his own brother. Not a warm and fuzzy story, but there's a point to it.

When Adam and Eve bit that apple, not only did *they* get infected with sin, but all of their offspring did too. (COVID-19 on steroids, all variants in play.) If you believe in the biblical account of creation as I do, then you would understand that *all* of us come from Adam and Eve — they are the ultimate parents of everybody. So, not only do we get the blessing of being at the top of the created order and the distinction of being made in the very image of God, we also get the sin component that we inherited from our original forbearers, Adam and Eve. It all flows downhill, doesn't it? Do you ever wonder why you do the things you don't want to do? Or where all the dark stuff in your heart comes from? Say hello to sin my friends, it's in the blood.

You came by it naturally, it's an inheritance ... a curse, if you will. Temptation never leaves, it's always lurking just around the corner, and as the Good Book says, sin just "lies at the door." Wow. It sounds like the fix is in, my lot is cast, and it's all over but the cryin'.

But wait. There's another way to look at it. Another option. Just because sin hangs around, that doesn't mean we have to ACT on it. It doesn't mean we must abide by it. Said another way, we have the choice to say "no" to sin. We can say "no" to the bad stuff, and "yes" to what's right. You and I *always* have a choice! Cain didn't do so well —but his story does *not* have to be our story.

Maybe you've been making lousy choices. Maybe like Cain, your countenance, your attitude, and your chip-on-the-shoulder outlook on life just suck. Then guess what? In God's plan, we can start over. We can move forward. We align with Him *first,* then with His help, we start making right choices. So, understand, although sin is in and around us, with God as our leader and Lord, sin need not *rule* us.

Stay tuned friends, it just gets better.

THE SECOND CHANCE

Adam had relations with his wife again; and she gave birth to a son, and named him Seth, for, she said, "God has appointed me another child in place of Abel, because Cain killed him." ²⁶ To Seth also a son was born; and he named him Enosh. Then people began to call upon the name of the LORD. (Genesis 4: 25-26)

While the aftermath of sin is brutal, as discussed, it is *not* irrevocable. God says we will keep going. And for Adam and Eve, there's another chapter. The story of the first family might have been over, maybe *should* have been over...but it wasn't. THAT'S GOOD NEWS! Note the last verse (v.26): "Then people began to call upon the name of the Lord." That's big. Huge, actually. The implication? Simple, but profound: GOD IS SUPPPOSED TO BE INVOLVED. Better yet, we *want* God to be involved! He is not "up there" while we are "down here." Oh no, God is right in the middle of everything. All of it. Good times, tough times, all kinds of times.

To be blunt, if the God I follow, pray to, worship, and spend time with is distant and unengaged in the here and now, then I'm not even sure I'm interested. I want and need a God who is in the trenches, a God who I *know* is sovereign, who will be right there with me, and who I can call on early and often. Thank *goodness* that people started to call on the name of the Lord.

That sets the tone for the rest of us.

GET IT RIGHT

This is the book of the generations of Adam. On the day when God created man, He made him in the likeness of God. ² He created them male and female, and He blessed them and named them "mankind" on the day when they were created. (Genesis 5:1-2)

Only two verses, but we can't miss this. We have to make *really* sure we have this part right. It says here Adam and Eve were made in the *image* of God.

The *image* of God, not *equal* to God. Here's the deal. Being made in the image of God is one thing. *Being* God is altogether different. Lots of people think there's not much difference between the two, but they're wrong. There's a ton of difference. For starters, we are the created, not the Creator. We didn't have anything to do with how we were made, or much less, anything else. We're not God, we are His likeness, His image...but we're not God. God is sovereign, we're not. God rules, we don't. The point — God has the ultimate control, we don't.

Further, I'm good, I'm really good, with where I fall in this food chain. But a lot of people — a LOT of people — are not good with it. While many of us may not say it, we want to run our own ship, make all our own decisions, rule our own world, and if anything, just have the Almighty lend us a hand now and then. Not how it works. He made me, He created me, and not only is His lordship over my physical design, but His lordship is also over my life design...provided I let Him. As mentioned before, and we'll say it over and over — we *always* have a choice. No forced legislation here. I'm at the place where I know, *I know,* that His lordship and leadership are beyond invaluable, and that by following His blueprint, I will have an opportunity to have the best possible life I can muster on this side of heaven. That's right, I have certifiably drunk the Kool-Aid. I don't need to try and reinvent the wheel. Leading a rebellious life — or just a life where God isn't relevant — wears out after a while. So, when I see verses that remind us that we are the workmanship, but not the designer, I am good with that! Bring it on sister, just bring it on. I'm beating on this hard because I really want you to come to the same conclusion. I want you to say, "Yeah — I want to follow God's lead. I want to have His involvement. I want to follow the path that He lays out. I want that!" That's what will motivate you and me to say yes to God —we just have to *want* it. Give it some thought, and let's keep going.

NOAH

⁵ The Lord saw how great the wickedness of the human race had become on the earth, and that every inclination of the thoughts of the human heart was only evil all the time. ⁶ The Lord regretted that he had made human beings on the earth, and his heart was deeply troubled. ⁷ So the Lord said, "I will wipe from the face of the earth the human race I have created— and with them the animals, the birds and the creatures that move along the ground—for I regret that I have made them." ⁸ But Noah found favor in the eyes of the Lord.

¹³ So God said to Noah, "I am going to put an end to all people, for the earth is filled with violence because of them. I am surely going to destroy both them and the earth. ¹⁴ So make yourself an ark of cypress wood; make rooms in it and coat it with pitch inside and out. ⁷ I am going to bring floodwaters on the earth to destroy all life under the heavens, every creature that has the breath of life in it. Everything on earth will perish. ¹⁸ But I will establish my covenant with you, and you will enter the ark—you and your sons and your wife and your sons' wives with you. ¹⁹ You are to bring into the ark two of all living creatures, male and female, to keep them alive with you. ²⁰ Two of every kind of bird, of every kind of animal and of every kind of creature that moves along the ground will come to you to be kept alive. ²¹ You are to take every kind of food that is to be eaten and store it away as food for you and for them."

²² *Noah did everything just as God commanded him. (Genesis 6: 5-9, 13-22)*

Tough passages, man. So, this is result of the sin that entered the picture a few hundred years prior to this. The ripple effects go on forever. Specifically, we have corruption. Apparently, a lot of it. So much that God regretted the idea of putting us on the planet to begin with. So, you have kids? I do; four of them. Regardless of the stress and strain of raising offspring, I don't believe there was ever a time when I said I'd just as soon not have them. Or better yet, wish they'd never been born. Not the case with this bunch in Genesis Chapter 6. It was bad — *really* bad. So bad that God said, it's got to stop. Game over, we're gonna try this again. We're gonna have a mother flood. The flood of all floods. Everything goes. Truly, we start over. So now we meet Noah.

A quick review on what Genesis said about the guy: "Noah found favor in the eyes the Lord,"² and "...Noah was a righteous man, blameless among the people of his time, and he walked faithfully with God."³ The takeaway from this: As stated, we always have a choice. Always! Noah chose to walk faithfully with God. You know what that means? The guy *wanted* to live with God and for God, and it didn't matter what the herd did. So back to the script. God says, "Everything goes, except you Noah. You and yours, you're going to build an ark, and you're going to put a bunch of animals

---

² Genesis 6:8

³ Genesis 6:9

on it, float around for the better part of six months, and let all this shake out." So, what does Noah do? Answer: He builds an ark.

Wow.

You know how much further along I would be if I'd lived for God and not for others over the better part of 50 years? If I'd graded myself on walking in step with the Father as opposed to seeking the approval of my fellow man...or woman? Noah was an individual that made a life choice to live with and for God, and if the friends, neighbors, co-workers, extended family, whoever, didn't do that, he didn't care. You know what God really would like to see from us? Some spiritual *backbone*, man. Take a stand for once, live like God *matters*, that's what God would love to see out of all of us.

There's a great life of purpose, meaning, peace, and joy out there, but for the love of God, act like you *want* it. That's what Noah did. He put his freaking flag up. Oh, and one other point: notice what the description didn't say — nothing about being "perfect," or "sinless," or anything else like that. The Bible did call him "blameless" with regard to everyone else, but that's different. That means his intentions were right, his motives were pure, his focus was on point. He had his head screwed on right.

That's what God wants from us. Perfection not required, don't have to test negative for sin; what God is looking for is good intent, motives, and focus. So where are you right now? You go with the culture, or you go with God? Is life all about following your instincts, or do you live for something higher? Call it man, what's your story?

I'll tell you mine: I get as tempted as anyone, I could be as pagan as anybody you've ever met — you have no idea — and probably influenced others to do the same — but guess what? I think it gets me nowhere. I think in the long run, it is not in my best interest, or anyone else's, so therefore, I don't! I go the other way — I seek to live a godly lifestyle, and furthermore, I want to be *passionate* about it.

So, while we're on the subject, let me ask you a question: Do you ever get genuinely enthused about living for God? Or rather, is it a chore? I'm not here to criticize or condemn, but it's a key question. If, at your core, you think — you *really* think — that living for God and wanting Him in your life gives you the best opportunity to live life to its fullest, you'll have some passion, some *drive*, for living God's way. If not, if you believe in God only because you just want to check the box and cover the bases, then honestly, I don't know if your faith will mean much to you. For me, it's easy. I absolutely think walking a godly path will give me the best opportunity to live a full life, a successful life, a joyful life, a complete life.

That's where Noah was. The guy made his choice. I think and I hope that over the next 20 years, I would want people to say that I had the right perspective, the right vision. I will stumble along the way, you and I both know we'll have bad hair days, but it doesn't matter. We get our heads and hearts in the right place, we move forward. It's your call. If you live for God and with God and believe He's got your best interests at heart, you'll be passionate about pursuing a relationship with Him. If not, He won't mean much to you and you'll go elsewhere to get your kicks.

THE REBOOT

4/2/24

[11] Now the earth was corrupt in God's sight and was full of violence. [12] God saw how corrupt the earth had become, for all the people on earth had corrupted their ways. [13] So God said to Noah, "I am going to put an end to all people, for the earth is filled with violence because of them. I am surely going to destroy both them and the earth. [14] So make yourself an ark..."

[3] and the water receded steadily from the earth, and at the end of one hundred and fifty days the water decreased.

[13] Now it came about in the six hundred and first year, in the first month, on the first of the month, the water was dried up from the earth. Then Noah removed the covering of the ark, and looked, and behold, the surface of the ground was dried up. [14] In the second month, on the twenty-seventh day of the month, the earth was dry. [15] Then God spoke to Noah, saying, [16] "Go out of the ark, you and your wife and your sons and your sons' wives with you. [17] Bring out with you every living thing of all flesh that is with you, birds and animals and every creeping thing that creeps on the earth, that they may breed abundantly on the earth, and be fruitful and multiply on the earth." [18] So

24

*Noah went out, and his sons and his wife and his sons'
wives with him. ¹⁹ Every beast, every creeping thing,
and every bird, everything that moves on the earth,
went out by their families from the ark.*

²⁰ *Then Noah built an altar to the L*ORD*, and took of
every clean animal and of every clean bird and offered
burnt offerings on the altar.* ²¹ *The L*ORD *smelled the
soothing aroma; and the L*ORD *said* [i]*to Himself, "I will
never again curse the ground on account of man, for
the intent of man's heart is evil from his youth; and I
will never again destroy every living thing, as I have
done.* (Genesis 6: 11-14; 8:3, 13-21)

So, there it is. God cleaned house. Just started over. If we take
the verses at their word, the earth was covered in water for
the better part of a year. That will do it. You know, sometimes we
need to start over too. We need a re-do. If you are reading this
and I've hit a chord, well, *thank goodness* you have time. Thank
goodness you have the opportunity for a reset. Whatever kind of
train wreck your life may have become, either through your own
choices or just bad luck, you and I *can* start over! You really need
to hear this.

There was a point in my past where I really didn't think that
was possible, but when that lie was busted wide open, the world
changed. I mean changed! So — you lose a fortune lately? You in
prison? I mean locked up literally, if not emotionally, financially,
or otherwise? Your marriage screwed up? Health turn to crap? I
got it sweetheart, I got it. And I don't flinch when I tell you again
— in God's hands, you get a do-over. You get another shot at it.
So, the simple fact is, as long as you can still read, or get read to,
and you're looking at and listening to this, you've avoided the
mother of all floods. Those poor people in Noah's day were beyond

redemption. You're not, and I'm not. What a relief! Trust me, I've started over a few times, and I'm just grateful I had the chance. So do you. Consider it a gift my friend...consider it a gift.

So, Noah starts again. He and his family of eight. And a lot of animals. The ark hits a mountain, the waters recede, and the do-over begins. Three points to make:

1. Noah had church. "Then Noah built an altar to the Lord."[4] It's the first thing he did when he got off the boat. Built an altar. Had a moment with God. What's the significance Noah knew, He *knew*, that the only reason he was where he was — and not buried under water like everyone else — was that God had spared him. And not only him, but his family as well. Noah is a thankful man. A grateful man. An appreciative man. A humble man. Someone who recognizes that God has been with him and taken care of him. You and I want to be there, too. Much, much better from a mental health standpoint to be grateful vs. not grateful .

2. God is in control. One more time: God is in control. I absolutely believe it. If He can cause a worldwide flood to hit, He can also keep it from happening again. There is a mindset out there that absolutely refuses to believe that God or anything or anybody can be *that* sovereign, *that* dominating, *that* far reaching. So, here's where I'm at. Not only do I believe it, but I think it takes a lot more faith, a lot more speculation to believe that the world and everything we know about it from the dawn of creation to this morning, is just...random. That there's no rhyme, no reason, no conclusion, no rationale, no trust in anything. Sorry — I just can't accept that. Oh, make no mistake: on

---

[4] Genesis 8:20

this side of heaven anything can happen, but that does not mean that God is not real, doesn't exist, or doesn't care.

Which leads me to my last point.

3. God feels. Notice: "The Lord...said in His heart: 'Never again will I curse the ground...'"[5] The operative phrase here — *in His heart.* Focus on that one. Here's the thing: If you think that life is just a product of chance happenings, fate, unseen forces, or whatever else you chalk up to how the world works....the bottom line is, none of those involve *hearts*. That means they don't care...they *can't* care. The universe doesn't have the capacity to love and care. It doesn't have a heart. However, the God of the universe absolutely *does care, does* love, and *does* feel.

So maybe your question is, "If He loves me so freaking much, why does all the bad crap happen?" Believe me, I get it. I'm not immune to it, either. I've had my share of crap to deal with; don't even get me started. As we've seen, we had a perfect world before sin entered the picture, and we've been dealing with the fallout ever since. But let me be crystal clear: that does *not* mean that God doesn't exist, or doesn't love, it just means we live in a world that can have some really high quality garbage in it.

Somehow, we have this idea that if God Almighty does exist and He's good, then He would make all the bad things go away. Or if He's loving, when we screw up, He would just pretend it never happened.

Really? So if you're a parent, you let your kids get away with murder and say it's all good? Do you say there's no right and

---

[5] Genesis 8:21

wrong, that it's all relative, that little Johnny or Jamie is completely justified in *whatever* they do? Probably not.

So, the picture gets clearer: God *is* here, He does care, but it doesn't change the fact that we live in a world that is marred and messed up by imperfections, at least on this side of heaven.

There *is* some very good news about all this, and we'll get to that — but for now, I want you to understand that God is here, and He cares, even in a world turned upside down. So, while I don't think it's likely, if I go broke, get beaten up, thrown in prison, my kids all hate me, I lose a leg, or end up under a bridge...I know I've got a God who loves me and cares about me. Even if my life is one big train wreck from this day forward, I know when I exit this place, I'll go to be with Him, and I have a future. I can live with that. I can bank on that, and that's one heck of a lot better plan than the other stories I hear out there. Seriously, you tell me if you have a better pitch.

Bottom line. God promised there wouldn't be another flood like the one Noah saw.

And guess what? There hasn't been.

The Plan

4/2/24

The LORD had said to Abram, "Go from your country,
your people and your father's household to the land
I will show you.

[2] "I will make you into a great nation,
and I will bless you;
I will make your name great,
and you will be a blessing. (Genesis 12:1-2)

So, God starts over with humanity, gives the human race another chance, and time passes. Generations come and go, and we get to the place where God says it's time to move this whole thing forward. To progress, if you will. Specifically, he says that out of all of the populace, He is going to create *a people*. Specifically, a line of people that will be His ambassadors to the rest of the world. A people that He can work through, a people He can lead, guide, direct, and develop. A people that will have a significant part to play in bringing us back into right relationship with Him.

Right relationship.

You see, when Adam and Eve ate the apple and sinned in the Garden of Eden, they didn't just lose their home in the Garden, they lost that right relationship with the Father. That was the biggest loss that occurred in this whole deal. Where we live and what we do is not the thing that defines us — having that right relationship with God is. So God, in His infinite wisdom and with an incredible amount of love, decides it's not enough to simply keep us alive and let us exist. He wants to bring us back to Himself. He says, I want them to have the chance, the opportunity, to get back to that beautiful place of relationship where they are in union with Me and I with them. The way it was supposed to be all along. That's where I want all this to end up.

And so, God has a plan. Round two. The sequel. God chooses a family to be the foundation by which He will gather men and women back to Himself. In military terms, He wants boots on the ground. He wants some people who will show the way; become examples, illustrations, leaders — and point the way back to Him. So, He chose a man named Abram. A couple of things here. First off, we don't know everything about Abram, or his wife Sarai, that would give us insight on why there were chosen. They just were. But here's the thing: God uses mainstream people to do miraculous things. There is nothing in all the Bible that says these two were special, unique, gifted, talented, or privileged. Please understand this. There is no privilege, rank, pedigree, or hierarchy in God's kingdom...none. He places no special value on any person, family, race, creed, status, looks, bloodline, religion, wealth, or any other category you come up with. Hear me on this: IN GOD'S EYES, WE ARE ALL EQUAL.

Right now, in my country we have all kinds of hell going on about injustice and inequality. Bad stuff. Lots of bad feelings about it. People have all kind of reasons for why it's there. What makes my blood boil is that some will blame God, or rather, they say that religion is part of the problem, and definitely not the solution. Let me tell you something; in God's economy, in God's plan for humanity, for kingdom living, for maximizing potential, for everything we can think of that's true and right, there is not (and has never been) any place for inequality, period. All the prejudice, the racism, the inequalities, the caste systems, formal and otherwise, all of that is our doing, not God's. If people really lived for God and the way He wanted, we would be examples of how to treat our fellow man and woman...nothing less would even be considered.

But back to our story. God picks Abram and Sarai, an ordinary couple from an ordinary family, living an ordinary life and doing ordinary things. God calls them out and gives them a part to play in His divine plan. And guess what? You and I also have a part to play. God doesn't pick and choose only special people for His assignments. Every one of us has a purpose, a plan, a part to play. That is not debatable. What *is* in question is whether you and I will embrace that fact. Make no mistake, God uses all of us, to this very day. You and I are created not just to watch football or sit in front a cell phone and thumb our lives away. *You* may have no clue what your life is about or where you're headed, but that's not because that plan isn't there.

So, God called Abram to make a nation that would be used to bring people to God. Nice. Good for him. The story here is that you and I have a calling as well. We all have things He would like us to do, to participate in. Even if you have no clue what that may be for you — He does. Honestly, whatever it is, it's secondary. What's primary is that we get in the flow with God. That's when life starts to harmonize. That's when light bulbs start to go on.

This is where it's at. You and I, no matter where we've been or where we're at, what we want is to be on the path. His path. Maybe you and I are supposed to be an encouragement to people that need it, cook something, read something, pay for something...man, I don't know, but what I *do* know is that we have our part to play. Candidly, I do think we have a self-esteem problem around here. Namely, an awful lot of people feel that they don't measure up. That others are more gifted, more talented, more superior, and just flat-out better candidates for whatever God has in mind. Let me help you with that, and I'll say it as gently as I can. It's crap. It's total crap. You and I have value. We have a purpose. God says so, and He made us, so *that* is what we take to the bank. Game on. No more "I don't count for anything." Don't want to hear it. Nobody's better, nobody's most favored, nobody's more loved more...it's all even. No doubt, some of us may get more headlines, but at the end of the day, we live with God and for God...and when we do, the rest of life takes care of itself.

The Response

So Abram went, as the LORD had told him; and Lot went with him. Abram was seventy-five years old when he set out from Harran. ⁵He took his wife Sarai, his nephew Lot, all the possessions they had accumulated and the people they had acquired in Harran, and they set out for the land of Canaan, and they arrived there. (Genesis 12:4-5)

These two verses pack a big punch. A big punch. Just take a look at the first three words of verse 4: "So Abram went ..." That's it. "So, Abram went." Monstrous passage. The implications are immeasurable. What's so big about it? It's simple: Abram *went*! He did what he was supposed to do! He was available, he said, "I'll go!" In other words, he showed up!

Let me tell you something about God and about life. Half the battle, half the challenge, half the victory is nothing more than showing up. You've heard that before, but nowhere is it more profound than in living a life with God. Our job is to show up. God's job is to lead. You think Abram and Sarai had all the answers about this new gig? Let me help you with a little context. God told them to leave mom and dad, leave the family, leave the known, and head out into the *unknown*. Literally. We're in the ancient Middle East about now. It's desert man, real honest-to-God desert. A lot of weird things and weirder people out there. And it's not like they had a posse to go with them. A few hired folks, that's about it. This was not comfortable; this was not a lay-up. So, Abram and Sarai had a choice to make. God gives the call; they have to accept it. I promise you they did not know the details. I guarantee you they didn't know exactly how this would play out. But man, they took the challenge. They said yes. You can see where I'm going with this: When we put ourselves in God's crosshairs and He starts positioning us, we are to respond! Come on! We respond! Sure, we won't know all the details in advance, but what we do know is that if He is leading, we're in good hands. You *have* to believe that. You have to buy in. If not, you got nothing.

Life is not meant to be lived alone.

He's with us. He's here. It may not feel like it at times, but that doesn't matter. He's right here. Right now. You book it. He says, we're gonna do this together. Trust me, Abram and Sarai didn't have all the answers about what God was going to do with them. No way. Trust me, they weren't anointed with extra amounts of wisdom, character, intelligence, perseverance, or courage...not all. But give credit where credit's due; they were obedient to the call. That was it.

That's the gig. Just show up. Do what we are led to do. Don't try to be something we're not, don't feel like we have to get a degree in something first...just show up! I wonder what might have happened if Abram had said, "No, I'm not going anywhere. Too risky, too 'out there,' too uncertain. I'm staying put." My take? God would have used somebody else, and Abram and Sarai would have missed out. They would have denied themselves the opportunity to be a part of God's plan. One key point here: if you think living for God is too mundane and pedestrian, then you've not yet lived for Him. Lots of times, at least initially, the world's way can look a lot sexier (not always, but a lot of the time), but what I will tell you from one who's tried both ways, living for God is not only just as good — it's *better*. More worthwhile, doesn't fade out, no hangovers, and it gets deeper and richer the longer we go with it.

So, I got excited about God in my late twenties...really felt I was on to something real. Now, 30+ years later, the intensity is even bigger. If my family thinks I'll eventually outgrow the thrill, it's doubtful at this point. And you know what? When we all gather 10 years from now, I will predict life will be more exciting, still! Age just seasons you in God's economy — no need for a mid-life crisis in this deal. We've always got something to look forward to, something to live for, so yeah, I'm too far gone now to change course.

And while we're on it, whatever else happens or doesn't happen to me; whether I end up rich as Caesar, poor as dirt, or something in between, whether I have great health, good looks, friends for days, or nothing remotely close, whatever I look like after it's all said and done — regarding God and His plan for my little life, I want to say *I showed up*. That's my deal, man. And sure, I want you to show up, too. Get in the game. Details to follow. Just get your head right and get in the game.

WHY THIS?

10 Now there was a famine in the land, and Abram went down to Egypt to live there for a while because the famine was severe. (Genesis 12:10)

So, Abram and his wife Sarai showed up. They did the right thing, the best thing. They put themselves out there — they're on the road. God's plan is at work. All's good...and now we get to a stress point. A moment of vulnerability, perhaps. A fear trap. So, to make sure we are all on the same page, let's set the stage.

While on the way to the place God promises to bring them — a place where they will become a people with historic impact and significance — we have a blip. Trouble on the road to paradise. To be specific, we have a famine. It's a problem. Running out of food is not good, and running out of food and water in the desert is worse. Maybe it's good in the sense that you'll die quicker, but you know, I'd rather at least have a shot at staying alive. Not in the desert my friend. Famine in the big sand box is *not* where you want to end up. By the way, do you know why the desert is the desert? You know why it's mainly a resort for coyotes, snakes, and tumbleweed? Because it's freaking brutal out there. Trust me, I know.

In my first life as a young Marine, I got stationed (sentenced, actually) to the beautiful garden hot spot known as 29 Palms. Sounds good, but it's a fabulous lie. It's really a code name for 972 square miles of Mohave Desert, where the Marine Corps trains for desert warfare. In February, you can get frost bite. In August, the heat can bust thermometers. I was 24 and looked 54. Your skin can double for sandpaper. So no, being stuck in a famine in the desert is not ideal. But that's where Abram and Sarai are. So why am I harping on all this? Because it's important, *really* important, to understand that even when we are on God's plan and path, there can be problems. Big problems. So sorry to burst your bubble — apologies for making the hard statements — but it is a fact, an absolute fact, that living with and for God does not exempt us from pain and suffering. To think we get an automatic "Get Out of Jail Free" card is just total delusion. Fake news, man. Not true truth.

It's so important that we get this right. Important because most people get turned off to God because the world didn't rotate right for them. The person we wanted to marry went the other way. The job that was so promising didn't deliver. Having great health from the cradle on didn't happen for us. You always suck at golf no matter how much you pray about it. Whatever the issue is, however it plays out, there are problems and there are setbacks. To deny this fact is just really bad theology. There is a view or a way of thinking that says if I've surrendered to God's leadership, live for him, and set out on the journey that He has for me and mine, somehow the calamities that happen to other people won't happen to me. I can't tell you enough times how wrong that is. Granted, you might avoid the self-induced or self-inflicted injuries, but problems can come whether you brought it on yourself or not. There is no God-bubble that insulates His followers from really bad stuff.

Honestly, I made it longer than most do before understanding how this worked. I was in my late 40's before the fat really hit the fan. For me, the first shot across the bow was watching my best buddy's wife die a slow death due to cancer at the ripe old age of 46, leaving him with three kids to raise. Truly, half the state of Texas was praying for her to be healed, and she believed God would absolutely do that, all the way up to the day she was gone. So where was God's favor in that mess? Did we not pray long enough, hard enough, or loud enough? Then it all just went downhill from there: in my own circles I saw suicides, financial crisis, depression, marriage issues with people that weren't supposed to have marriage issues, kid issues, health issues, career issues — all to GOOD people! Godly Christian people, sweet people, giving people, caring people, loving people. So, what is *that* all about?

We'll get there, but first, back to the script, to the bigger story. Abram and Sarai are in a famine, in the desert. And it's a problem. So, here's the punch line my friend — welcome to the world! That just it — welcome to the freaking world! When it's been my turn and I've been thrown into some of the quagmires of life, I've thought that I was the only one. As in, "Really, God, was that absolutely necessary? Was I *that* bad in my prior life to get all this poured on me? I mean, Hitler was worse...wasn't he? So why me Lord — why *me*? But now, a few gray hairs later, I've come to believe that if people have made it to 50 without the world going sideways on them in some way, truly, they are the exception, *not* the norm.

Most people I know have had it handed to them in some way...and my story — or your story — may be better or worse. But bottom line, we've *all* had some famines to go through. You'd think that God's point couple in Genesis might get a break, but no, not even these two are exempt from the pains that life can bring. The good news is, there is upside to all of it, but for now, we need to understand that this stuff just happens. It's for real, and we need to get our arms around it.

Before we leave all this, we have one more issue to discuss. Notice the famine that found Abram and Sarai was "severe." So severe that Abram and Sarai decide to take a detour. The Bible says they went to Egypt "to live there for a while." Some say this was Abram's first mistake. Specifically, God had a plan for them to go to Canaan, the land He promised. Where it's all gonna happen. And there was no footnote that said, let's go wait out the famine in Egypt. So why did they go down there? If God says, "Go till I say stop," then *go*, dude. Why the blink? Egypt? Really? Your God is bigger than famines man, where in the world is your faith, where is your belief, your conviction? Sure, in famines in the desert you die faster, but still, God is on your side. Maybe so, Abram must have reasoned. But then there's the other side. Let's discuss this like rational people. Egypt has food and water. We are running out of both, at the moment.

It was appropriate, logical, and right for them to seek shelter, wasn't it? Honestly, why are we even debating this? They didn't say they weren't going to where God wanted them to go; nobody's talking about Plan B, they're just trying to make decent decisions. If God gives us a brain, He expects us to use it, right? We are rational, reasonable, intelligent creatures — not hippos or rhinos or anything else that runs on instinct, correct? So, who's right? All the verse says is that they had a bad famine, so they went to Egypt to get relief. So, was that the right call? Guess what — the Bible doesn't say. We will never know whether what Abram and Sarai did was right or wrong. So, what's the point? When we live with and for God, there will be situations like this for all of us. Do you keep this job, or is there something better? Do you move or do you stay put? Do you draw the line with your spouse on this issue, or let it go...maybe for now, maybe forever? Do your kids stay in that school, or do they go elsewhere? Do you stay in this town, this church, this community, this county, this state, or do you do something different? Just give me the blasted *answer,* man, so we can all get on with our lives!

Let me help you with this. Sometimes, I don't know and you don't know. Doesn't that make you feel better? That's all I've got. I know I feel better now — how about you? No need to ask further questions; that just settles it. We don't know. Won't know. But for those of us who might have a few more questions, let me share a couple of things. For starters, not knowing whether to turn left or right doesn't just happen to Bible people like Abram and Sarai. You know it happens to us too. Another great pearl of wisdom for you: there *will* be situations, circumstances, and issues that arise, and you won't know the exact route to take.

In my little world, I can say that most of the time I have a sense of direction on things, but there have been times when I just wasn't sure. At all. I *think* so, I *feel* so, but don't *know* so. It could be a work issue, a parenting issue, a health issue...but whatever it is, there's a question mark. Here's the key: no matter what I feel, what I think, what I know or don't know — I want God to be involved. Did you get that? One more time: I *want God to be involved*. No question about it; I want Him to be in on everything. You feeling me yet? Everything!

I have prayed about everything from who I should marry, how to raise kids, how I should work, who I should work with, where I should live, what house I should buy, how I spend money, what church I attend, what causes I support, how I spend my time, who I vote for, what barbecue pit I get, and whether or not I should buy the Harley or the Honda. Whatever the issue, I want God involved. I want Him in *everything*. I want Him out front, in the foxhole, in good times, rough times, in-between times. I want Him involved. So, would I have gone to Egypt? I don't know. What would *you* have done? I guarantee you this: if we could take a poll, some would say no and some would say yes. So understand: When the answer is not as clear cut as we'd like it to be, you want God to be involved. He wants to be involved too, by the way, but He won't force Himself on you. It's your call, your choice.

I've learned well enough that I want His leadership in every aspect of my life. I'm not going to get sidetracked. If He's in my life it *will* work out, and I'm not going to sweat whether or I not

I go to Egypt. I'll ask, I'll pray, and I'll make the best decision I know how to make. If I'm in His will, if I've given Him the reins over my life, I can move forward knowing that He ultimately will have His way, and my life will work out as it should. If I zigged when I should have zagged, He can still get me where I need to go. Same for you. So, you do the best you can with what you got.

THE BLINK

As he was about to enter Egypt, he said to his wife
Sarai, "I know what a beautiful woman you are.
¹²When the Egyptians see you, they will say, 'This is
his wife.' Then they will kill me but will let you live.
¹³Say you are my sister, so that I will be treated well
for your sake and my life will be spared because of
you." (Genesis 12:11-13)

Houston, we have a problem. The good news: Sarai is really good looking. The bad news: Sarai is really good looking. I didn't do a deep dive into the story, but it's pretty well understood that back in the day, if you're a king, the man in charge, one of the perks is that you pretty much get what you want. Comes with the territory. Could be land, could be cattle, could be women...whatever. Regarding the latter, it's not a problem if the woman you want is in a committed relationship — when you're the king you can fix that, easy. Regarding the current husband, it's get lost or get dead; we can help you with either.

Knowing all this, Abram takes stock of the situation and thinks, "My wife is hot. This could be a problem." So here comes the blink: "Hello, Mr. King of Egypt. Nice to meet you, and it's great to be here! I'm Abram, and this is my *sister* Sarai."

So sure enough, the "sister" play seems to work! Pharaoh treats Abram well for Sarai's sake, and Abram comes away with sheep and cattle, male and female donkeys, male and female servants,

and even male and female camels. Splendid! This is going wonderfully well...better than expected. Abram not only has his life intact, but he's getting benefits as well — the fact that his wife is no longer with him seems a bit irrelevant at this point. But to make sure you have full context, please read on to verse 15: "... and she was taken into his palace." You know where that leads, right? She wasn't taken into the palace to have breakfast and talk about desert life or the pyramids ....no, no, no, she was taken into the palace to become a part of Pharaoh's personal club — The Harem Club, to be exact. She is now part of the female posse. On the one hand, the benefits are attractive: great food, plenty to drink, cool in the summer and warm in the winter, looking and feeling good the whole time...because that is what is expected. It's expected because it's part of the job description: that you are available and on call 24/7 to provide "personal services" to The Man. Whenever, wherever, you are on speed dial whenever Mr. Big says he'd like to spend some time and get to know you better. We're talking companionship on demand. Better yet , *sex* on demand, and it's been going on for thousands of years folks. To be fair , we don't know *for sure* that our heroine had to go that far with The Man , but I'm just sayin, that's the tradeoff for the perks.

One point of interest here: nowhere do we hear anything about Abram's state of mind. Was he grieving? Was he angry? Upset? Heartbroken? At the very least, was he sad at all, or maybe just relieved that he still breathed fresh air and his head was still on his shoulders? You know what I think? Just speculation on my part, but I think he just felt resigned. Yep. Resigned. Resigned to the fact that he made the decision to go to Egypt. Resigned to the fact that his wife was too good looking, and that he lied about their marital status. Resigned to the fact that he was not in a position to go toe to toe with Pharaoh. He's just resigned to it all. It is what it is. But hey, at least he's alive...and got some stuff out of it to help pad the pocketbook. As for that plan of starting a great nation, being a part of history, doing something no one has ever done, well, it was exciting to think about. But real life is real life, and so, while it all sounded good, let's face it — nice thought, but it's apparently not going to happen. At least not by Abram's hand. But God had other plans:

> But the LORD inflicted serious diseases on Pharaoh and his household because of Abram's wife Sarai. So Pharaoh summoned Abram. "What have you done to me?" he said. "Why didn't you tell me she was your wife? Why did you say, 'She is my sister,' so that I took her to be my wife? Now then, here is your wife. Take her and go!" Then Pharaoh gave orders about Abram to his men, and they sent him on his way, with his wife and everything he had.[6]

This is almost comical. I don't know how it all went down, but what I *do* know is that suddenly we had trouble in paradise. Bad karma for Pharaoh and company. Don't know what the diseases were, don't know how long they stayed, how much they hurt, but I know this: it was God's way of letting Pharaoh know there was a problem at home, and he needed to fix it, and fix it quick. Namely Pharaoh, you're about to do something *really* bad with someone's wife (a clue, this woman is *not* his sister!), and it's gonna get dark fast for you and yours unless you get her (and Abram) out of your world — now!

Folks, this is God at work. When He has a plan, He has a plan...period.

The fact that Abram saw no way out of his circumstances did not mean that God didn't have answers — what it meant is that Abram didn't see them. So, let me help you with something really

---

[6] Genesis 12: 17-20

critical here, really important. The sooner you get this right, the better your life will be. Specifically, GOD DOES NOT HAVE TO TELL US HOW HE WORKS.

One more time: GOD DOES NOT HAVE TO TELL US HOW HE WORKS.

You get that? If you get nothing else out of this whole story, get your arms around the fact that God will many times, even *most* times, not give us the play-by-play on how He operates. Get that, and you my friend, are on your way.

So, let's get back to it. If we armchair quarterback this thing, I think the right thing was for Abram to tell the truth. He could have avoided a lot of hassle, a lot of stress. And let's be *very* clear here — it wasn't all about Abram. It was about Sarai. *She* was the one facing a life as a sex kitten to a foreign king she didn't know and probably didn't like. She was the one being thrown under the bus. No, the lesson here is pretty clear to me: you just do the right thing. Every time. Do the right freaking thing.

If you've brought it to God, and you've said He leads, He will. You and I don't need to help him out and fudge the numbers, play fast and loose with the truth, or define integrity as we see fit. There's a verse in the New Testament that says, "If God is for us, who can be against us?" Real good verse, too. Take it literally. It doesn't mean a red carpet gets laid out for us everywhere we go, but it *does* mean that God is in control, He's ultimately BIGGER than our circumstances, He will navigate us through this little life of ours, and we will be the better for it.

Abram's lucky he didn't get his head handed to him —- liter-ally — for lying to the big man. I think all of it could have been avoided, had he just done the right thing from the start. How about you and I do the right thing from the start? For a lot of us, it will take time to get that down. We're so used to working off our reflexes that we'll have to slow it down, pray it through, and see how God might lead. It will take time. Trust me, I know. *Still* learning how to do the right thing all the time. I'm better at it now, and should be even better a week, a month, and a year from now.

You never retire from learning to do the right thing. You just get better at it. You get *stronger.* Living by fear, living by reflex — *not* the way we go through life. So, no more blinking for us — we're gonna stare straight ahead, keeping our eyes on Him. Let's take that verse *really* literally: "If God be FOR us, who can be against us?" Get that down, you're on the right path. You'll feel better, look better, and probably sleep better, too.

One Issue

After this, the word of the Lord *came to Abram in a vision:*

"Do not be afraid, Abram.
 I am your shield,
your very great reward.¹"

But Abram said, "Sovereign Lord, *what can you give me since I remain childless and the one who will inherit my estate is Eliezer of Damascus?" And Abram said, "You have given me no children; so a servant in my household will be my heir."*

Then the word of the Lord *came to him: "This man will not be your heir, but a son who is your own flesh and blood will be your heir." He took him outside and said, "Look up at the sky and count the stars — if indeed you can count them." Then he said to him, "So shall your offspring be."*

Abram believed the Lord, *and he credited it to him as righteousness. (Genesis 15:1-6)*

There's going to be a whole lot more to this episode as we move forward, but regardless, a precedent has been set here that's critical for us to understand. The Lord is promising to Abram that he *still* has a huge part to play in God's plan to redeem humanity. Namely, God is planning to build a nation of people through him; a nation that is meant to be a light to the rest of the world...a nation that will point the way back to God — we are talking *the chosen ones*. I mean, this is big, *monstrously* big. Probably nothing bigger since God made Adam and Eve. This is the plan to bring us back to God. This is where it's all gonna start, and our Abram and Sarai, that sweet little couple out of the land of Ur, they're gonna forge the path for all the rest of us. The buck *starts* with them. A freaking nation, man. What couple starts a nation? So, there it all is — the stage is set.

One problem. Just a small issue. I hate to get in the way of a good story and all this momentum, but something needs to be said. Not to be a Debbie Downer, but Abram and Sarai, well, they don't have a kid. Not even a step kid. They have a nephew, Lot, but he's no longer around. So as far as Abram is concerned, the only available heir is one of his staff members; Eliezer, a servant from Damascus to be specific. You see, to have a nation built out of you, the rational mind says you start with a family. A family with kids. Offspring! Then, those kids have kids, *those* kids have kids, and this whole thing starts to multiply. Do you see how it works? And so, the logical premise is that we would have a family unit to begin all this off-springing and build out the linage. That's how you build a nation.

But Abram and Sarai — no kids. Not even one. No go on the babies, man — nothing. So maybe it's not their time yet. Maybe Sarai will get pregnant tonight. Maybe it just takes longer for them. I mean, really, out of our 4 kids, we had a delay from kid 1 to kid 2 of like, I don't know, 3 years? Then all of a sudden, it happened. Voila! So maybe that happens here. Well, you see, we *could* take that approach, but that might not be the case here, simply for the fact that they have been trying for *50 years* to have a kid, and...nothing!

This dude Abram is around 80 years old, and sweet Sarai is clocking in at a not-so-fertile 70. Do you see the challenges this presents? We're talking as dry a well as there ever could be. Nothing happening here sweetheart — there are no offspring in the works. God says there's a nation to be birthed out of you — He says that you'll have more descendants than Florida has sand (or retirees) — but well, the fact is, we don't have even *one* heir on the ground at this point. Call it either comical or cruel, but that's where we are.

So many times, you and I only work off what we *see.* Abram sees that there is no kid coming. He sees that he and Sarai are not getting any younger. He sees that the only possible way a nation comes through him is by a servant (a one off if you will — BWG — Best We Got). And you know, like our man Abram, most of the time, most *all* of the time, we make decisions by looking at what is in front of us. What we can see, feel, quantify, get our arms around, however you want to say it — using all the information we can identify; that's how we make our choices and decisions. And I would tell you that for most part, there's nothing wrong with that — it's just common sense. But there are times, other times, when what we see, hear, feel and touch *doesn't add up.*

To hit it harder, situations arise where we don't see the angle, the possibility, what's even *doable,* much less an answer. There is just no way out, no thought that is within the realm of possibility, nothing we can plan or do to derail the upcoming train wreck. *That's* the worst. Along with that is the issue of control — or should I say, lack of it? The job is ending, financial markets are melting, the spouse has gone certifiably nuts — whatever. I've beaten this poor horse enough, but I say it all to get to the point. When it all has hit the fan and/or we are in complete free fall — or will soon be — what is the biblical response? Look at our guy:

"Abram believed the Lord, and he credited it to him as righteousness." Say hello to *faith*.

Faith.

Just faith.

Simple, honest to goodness, home grown , grassroots, unaltered, non-GMO, hormone free, purified *faith*.

We've all heard the word. In songs, athletic speeches, calls to arms, presidential messages, and church talk. Everybody's heard the word...*but* — very few know what it is...how it's applied...what it's worth and what it does. It's a shame, because at the end of the day, faith is at the very core of what God wants from us. If you don't have faith, you don't get far in your experience with God. If you don't have faith, you don't *use* faith, your relationship with God with be bittersweet at best, non-existent at worst.

Faith is the fuel for moving forward with God, growing with God, trusting God, and living with God. Sad to say, I've been a Bible teacher for over a quarter century, a real pro, and only until very recently have I started, *started*, to understand what faith is. I've missed out on a lot of peace, comfort and joy that could have been there, because if you don't have faith, you don't have much. Many believe in God and want to go to heaven, but in the here and now, God doesn't matter. So, if nothing else, we're going to get some Faith Training today. The buck stops here. Congratulations! You've arrived at Faith Training Day. Maybe we'll give out certificates if you pass.

To initiate the dialogue, before we understand how to have faith, or use faith, we have to know what faith *is* and *isn't*. Faith is not some something passive, something static, or something you own. It's certainly not something that can be bought, exchanged, or given. It's something you *do*. When it comes to faith in the Almighty, the word faith comes down to one simple statement of belief. Three words. No Hebrew, Greek, or Latin here. I'm suggesting a three-word sentence that your toddler can pick up.

GOD'S GOT THIS.

Again, for emphasis:

GOD'S GOT THIS!

One more time:

GOD'S GOT THIS!

So, what does that mean? It means exactly what it says — the simple plain truth that, whatever the circumstance, issue, challenge, or trial, God's got this. Period. Selah. Stick a fork in it. Game on, game over. It's done. When you say, "God, I want you in my life, I want You to lead my life, and I want You to matter in my life," then you have to say, regarding *everything* about your life — God's got this. And when you say, God's got this, and really mean it, guess what friends and neighbors? You, yes, *you* — are living by faith. That is the deal. You are living by faith. So, let's get real practical here. Let's do a little grunt work to make sure we understand how this works. Here's what it looks like:

> I'm concerned about my health. Faith says, "God's got this!"

> Concerned about money. Faith says, "God's got this!"

> Concerned about relationships or lack thereof. Faith says, "God's got this!"

> Concerned about a kid or a parent. Faith says, "God's got this!"

Concerned about a job. Faith says, "God's got this!"

Concerned about your desires and feelings. Faith says, "God's got this!"

Concerned about where you live, who you're married to, what your future looks like, what the doctor's report says, what that pain is about, all this anxiety that you have, the weather, your looks, your weight, your dog (I don't do cats), your summer, your fall, tennis, golf, marathons, holidays, cash flow, age, bad knees, pandemics, China, political parties, career change, prison, out of prison, college, high school, *any* school, parents, grandparents, neighbors from hell, kids from hell, *whatever* from hell...guess what? Faith says — all together choir — "God's got this!" I swear, I need to make bumper stickers and t-shirts that say that . That, my friends, is faith. Just straight up, black coffee, no cream, no sugar, fast-ball-over-the-plate, big time *faith*.

So back to our story. Let's look at God's message to Abram one more time.

"The man [Eliezer] will not be your heir, but a son who is your own flesh and blood will be your heir." Then it gets even better: "Look up at the sky and count the stars — if indeed you can count them. So shall your offspring be." Almost sounds like a tease, doesn't it? Some might say a not so funny joke. A little humor, at Abram and Sarai's expense. But through that, look how Abram responded: "Abram believed the Lord, and He credited it to Him as righteousness."

Ladies and gentlemen, we have a winner! A bombshell verse. It's one for the ages. You see, what Abram did was exercise faith. Notice I said *exercise*. Sometimes that's exactly what it is. It's work to exercise faith. You ever work out in your life? Run, lift, swim, row, stretch or climb? Something that caused you to push? Same thing here. In some cases, a lot of cases, we have to work at faith.

To be clear, faith is defined as "...confidence in what we hope for and assurance about what we do not see,"[7] Here's the deal: faith can sometimes be flat out countercultural. It's just not the norm. Culture says there are times when worry is appropriate. The biblical response says *don't worry about anything.*[8]

Faith says, "I don't have a freaking clue as to how this (whatever *this* is) is going to play out, but I know God is in it and ultimately God wins, so I will be the better for it. That, my friends, is faith. Just because I have no answer to my "this" doesn't mean there isn't one, it means I don't know what it is. Faith is the exact opposite of worry. Let me ask you a question: Did you ever worry your way to happiness? Did you actually worry enough about something that you finally squeezed an answer out of it? Me either. Nowhere do I read where worry is good. No, worry can kill people. But the culture, our upbringing and our friends and family say we're *supposed* to worry. That we care only if we worry. Genesis says, don't worry, have faith. Expect an answer. Expect a solution. Expect an outcome that helps you and honors God. Say, "Even though I don't know God's plan, I know he *has* one, and that's good enough for me."

And then you know what you do? Go get a good night's sleep. When you can go to bed in a firestorm saying, "God's got this," and get a good night's sleep in the middle of it, *then* my friend, you are getting somewhere. You don't have any faith today? Let not your heart be troubled. I didn't have much either. Guess what? We can grow it, we can build it, we can practice it...and you know what? It *will* come. Trust me, *trust me* — it will come! This isn't being a Pollyanna or just having a cheerleader attitude, this is the real deal man — *faith* is available when we let God in.

---

[7] Hebrews 11:1

[8] Philippians 4:6

So, here's the plan: right now, I want you to stop reading, and think about the biggest thing that's eating you up right now. What is it? For me, it's always the money, and thinking that I'm not the man my grandfather or my uncle was; the fear of *not measuring up*. Being unaccomplished, my friends. Hearing, "He had potential, but just never put it all together...such a shame." So, each and every day I will pray, "God, you have this, and it will be good, however it plays out." Then I'll go have a decent day and look to get a good night's sleep. And I suggest you do the same.

The fact that you don't *feel* it is immaterial. Just pray it. If you keep praying it and saying it, your faith *will* start to grow. Nothing sexy, miraculous, or incredible about it. Just a day-by-day slog. You provide the attitude; God provides an answer. It may be quick, or it may take time; doesn't matter which. That's how the game is played.

There's more to say, but we start now, in *faith*.

It's Never Free

Now when the sun was going down, a deep sleep fell upon Abram; and behold, terror and great darkness fell upon him. Then God said to Abram, "Know for certain that your descendants will be strangers in a land that is not theirs, where they will be enslaved and oppressed for four hundred years. But I will also judge the nation whom they will serve, and afterward they will come out with many possessions. As for you, you shall go to your fathers in peace; you will be buried at a good old age. Then in the fourth generation they will return here, for the wrongdoing of the Amorite is not yet complete." (Genesis 15:12-16)

Lest you and I doubt that we follow an incredible God — lest you and I *forget* —this passage gives us a snapshot of what He knows and how He operates.

I'm a glass half full guy. How about you? Actually, I want you to believe that I'm *more* than a glass half full guy. How about three-quarters full? Can I go four-fifths full? That to me is a much better way to live than going the half-full route. And my reason for being on the sunny side up? Ever since I realized God was here and God cared, that there was hope, a plan, and a direction for my life, I got lit up. How could I not? But I also know, looking back over 30-odd years with Him, it's not been all glamour and glitz, all milk duds and popcorn. Not only have I not gotten rich overnight, but I also haven't gotten rich, period. I feel like there is far more I have *not* accomplished than what I have accomplished .. My marriage has not been one continuous honeymoon. (Whose has?) I was so bad at golf I had to divorce the game. And by the time I can travel, I may be too old to care.

But wait — that doesn't fit. Isn't the story, when it's all God, it's all good? Isn't that how this is supposed to play out? Isn't that the pitch? If not, then what am I in this for?

Okay. So, here's the deal: more times than not, life will have difficulty. I don't care who you are, what you believe, or what your preconceptions are — the simple fact is, life is more than likely going to have some hardship. That's part of the ride. It can be on a micro- or a macro-scale, but bottom line, pain is pain, hardship is hardship, and it exists on this side of heaven.

Now, to be clear, living rightly related to God will help you and I avoid some self-inflicted wounds, but some of this stuff, well, we had nothing to do with it. So, what is the point? Folks, I know, I *know*, that living with and for God is the better way to go, whether my life lights up the scoreboard or not. Take my career. Man, I'm working on some things, and I hope we blow it out of the water. Just crush it. Maybe I can a write a book called *How I Did It* and they'll have me on the talk shows. Or not. Or maybe I never pop the long ball. I will climb the hill and climb it hard, but the simple fact is, there's no guarantee. There is no guarantee my kids will love me and come visit often. No guarantee my health stays strong. No guarantee I'll live where I want, do what I want (or *think* I want), accomplish anything over and above what I've done to date. No guarantees on any of it. But this I *do* know: whether life is hard or less hard from here — I know I'm better off with God. I *know* it!

I don't have to have the house on the hill or millions in the bank to say God's blessed me — just knowing I'm His and am living in some semblance of right relationship with Him is good enough. He brings me peace, He brings me hope, He brings me joy, and He brings me a future. *That* is good enough. So yeah, it's not so uplifting to see that this great nation God promised will spend the first 400 years in bondage and slavery. There's no feel-good there. But at the end of the day, God's plan is God's plan. That nation *will* emerge. They will not only survive, but they will also thrive, and God will be with them in and around and through all of it.

So, our man Abram is just a guy trying to get by, do what God wants him to do. He's been told he'll father a baby and from that baby a family, then a lineage, then a nation, and if that weren't enough, we get the dream that says that nation will be *slaves*. For 400 years. Wow. Poor Abram and Sarai are just living it out day by day, but God sees things hundreds, no, make it *thousands* of years down the road. We don't, but He does. We're called to do our part. He'll do His.

You and I want that! You and I want to know there is a hill to climb, a path to take, a direction to follow, and that it involves a legacy way bigger than what we see. Sure, I'd prefer the ride to be smoother than being in bondage all my life. Who wouldn't? But if that's the story, then in the hands of a living God, I am covered. He does have my back. If I don't see it in this life, then most assuredly I will in the one on the *other* side. There's a whole lot more on that statement than what we have time for, but just understand that with God, there is more — much more — than what we can see. Just know that.

A TWIST

*Now Sarai, Abram's wife, had not borne him a child,
but she had an Egyptian slave woman whose name
was Hagar. So Sarai said to Abram, "See now, the
LORD has prevented me from bearing children. Please
have relations with my slave woman; perhaps I will
obtain children through her." And Abram listened to
the voice of Sarai. And so after Abram had lived ten
years in the land of Canaan, Abram's wife Sarai took
Hagar the Egyptian, her slave woman, and gave her
to her husband Abram as his wife. (Genesis 16:1-3)*

Despite God's promise, all Abram and Sarai are doing is getting older. That's it. No pregnancy. No kid. No *hint* of a kid.
Nothing. So, the idea of starting a nation...well, God said it would
happen, but it hasn't. Maybe, possibly, it's time to look at Plan
B. It's time for action — time to help God out. Time to devise a
strategy, get creative, use our minds. After all, God gave us minds,
did He not? Well, Sarai has a great idea, a *super* idea! She sees
quite clearly that her biological clock has long since timed out;
her husband is 86 and she's right behind him at 76. Apparently
having a baby the old-fashioned way is not going to happen.

So what does she do? Sarai calls for backup . Specifically, the
hired help, a servant girl named Hagar. Her personal attendant,
to be exact. She's been part of the entourage the whole time —
living the dream right along with them until one day it dawns on

Sarai: Could it be — *could it be?* Could the real answer to fulfilling God's destiny for Abram and Sarai be right in front of them and they just didn't see it? I don't know a lot about Hagar, but this I do know: she was healthy, she was young, and she was available. I mean, all things considered, it's the ideal solution:

Sarai: "Abram, we've been waiting forever, and it's very clear that the magic with you and me isn't going to cut it. So, we're gonna tweak the plan a bit. Specifically, you are going to sleep with Hagar. Yep. Hagar. She's here, she can bear offspring, and she works for us, so she'll do what we say if she knows what's good for her. Granted, this may not be our first choice, but under the circumstances, it's the only alternative we've got, so get busy and make it happen!"

Abram: "Sure."

So, there you go. Abram slept with Hagar, and she conceived. Beautiful. We're done here. No more waiting on God. Mission accomplished: a baby is on the way! Sometimes you just have to take matters into your own hands, right? No disrespect to the Almighty, but there are simply times when you have to do what you have to do — take the bull by the horns — and clearly, this is one of those times. Or is it? Because it doesn't take long for the plot to thicken:

> *...when Hagar became aware that she had conceived, her mistress was insignificant in her sight. So Sarai said to Abram, "May the wrong done to me be upon you! I put my slave woman into your arms, but when she saw that she had conceived, I was insignificant in her sight. May the* Lord *judge between you and me." But Abram said to Sarai, "Look, your slave woman is in your power; do to her what is good in your sight."*

So Sarai treated her harshly, and she fled from her presence.[9]

Oh boy — here we go. Woman on woman. Women wars. We're in it now. Lest you missed anything, we've got a servant girl, a girl who does *not* have equal standing with the man and woman of the household, so at the end of the day she is hired help. But now, thanks to Sarai's plan, things have changed. *Hagar* is the one who is with child, not Sarai. *Hagar* is the one who will bring an heir into this world, Sarai will not. Back in those days, one of the ways a woman was valued was by her children, namely, how many she had, and in particular how many *boys* she had, because boys carried on the family name. I'm not saying it was right, but that's how it was. So now, in a twist of fate, our girl Hagar suddenly has the upper hand. She is holding the ace and apparently, she lets Sarai know about it. That, my friends, was not supposed to happen! That little end-around was never in the original playbook. I'm sure Sarai never saw it coming: *Where did that attitude come from? She works for me! She's not supposed to do that! This is upside-down.*

So, what does Sarai do? Well, she blames Abram!

Sarai: Now look what you've done! Not only is my maid pregnant, but she also thinks she's better than me! She's holding it over me, and you know what? It's your fault. Not only did you sleep with her, you got her pregnant!

Abram: Uhhh, excuse me, wasn't this your plan?

Sarai: Shut up! I'm worse off now than I was before, and it's all because of you! For your sake, you'd better find a way to fix this, or you just signed up for 20 years of wife pain !

Abram: Wow.

The joys of marriage.

---

[9] Genesis 16: 4-6

So here we are. While trying to help God and further the cause, we've just made a bigger mess out of the whole thing. Sure enough, Hagar has that baby. And congrats, it's a boy! Ishmael's the name. However, we have family strife. You ever done that? You ever been following a track, a plan, an agenda, and then, for no other reason than losing patience, got discouraged, became frustrated with the process and then you quit? Or you decided to go another direction? Like Abram and Sarai, did you take matters in your own hands — just say, "I gotta do what I gotta do." Forget whether God's in it or not..."I gotta do what I gotta do." You ever done that? Thought so. I have too. So let me help you with that.

Point #1: As a follower of God, just like Abram and Sarai — just like them — there is a plan for your life and mine. Make no mistake, there *is* a plan for your life and mine. It may not be to start a nation at retirement age, but that doesn't matter. What does matter is that God has a plan — or maybe *direction* is another good word — and He wants us engaged with Him in that direction.

Point #2: It's God's direction and God's timing, not ours. Granted, this is a tough one — a *real* tough one. Matter of fact, this is one that we struggle with the most. This is the one that can blow us up on a dime. Let me drop a pearl of wisdom on you. Most of us are *not* patient people. We do not like to wait. For many of us, "wait" is just a 4-letter word that does not mean good things. We want results, we want action, and if enough time goes by and we don't see it, we *will* do something about it. We want activity, we want direction, we want results and we want them now!

I wish I could put some lipstick on this. I really want to tell you how to fast track God's plan for your life, but the simple fact is, I can't. God works in us and with us in the way *He* wants, and the sooner we accept this, the better off we will be.

Point #3: If God isn't carrying out His plan as fast as you'd like, if you are frustrated and strung out waiting for things to happen, there's a really good possibility that He wants you to learn or to experience other things in the meantime. In my case, He wants me to grow. To develop. To get stronger. To mature. (I'm already 63 — how much more maturity do I need?) Let me give you an example.

As stated, my day job is in the business world. I'm approaching 34 years of doing what I do. To a certain degree, I could be considered successful, but just between us girls, I do not believe I've reached my full potential. When I tell you I'm still climbing the hill, that's *exactly* what I'm doing: climbing the hill and climbing it hard. To be frank, one of the reasons I climb so hard is because I do not believe I have accomplished all that I can. To be even more frank, I feel like I'm not where I *should* be, at least in *my* mind.

And then what's worse, just as I'm starting to get into my *seventh* decade of life (I mean, really — you know anyone older than me? Santa Claus? Your mom? *Anyone?*), I am only now realizing that I may, *may* — not live forever. To be brutally honest, I may only have another 10 years left to work at this, and you know what? I'm running out of time to make it right. So, like Sarai and Abram were running out of time regarding kids, I'm running out of time regarding work — there is simply not enough of it left. Instead, there's pressure. Strain. Anxiety. Fear. I'm not where I'm supposed to be, doing what I'm supposed to be doing. Sweet, precious Mother of God, *I am not going to make it!*

But wait. *Wait.*

God *did* say He has a plan for my life. He describes it in other places as "a future and a hope." But here's what you have to know: As stated, he doesn't provide all the details. Frankly, in my experience, He offers very little detail. Most of the time the directive is, we wait, we listen, we're open, we learn, we trust, we focus, and we *grow.*

While we're on it, I'll tell you another thing. Most, if not all the time, you and I are much more interested in results than in relationship. Specifically, we want what God can offer more than we want *Him*. (Developing a relationship takes time, and well, that's just not what we really want.) Any of you have teenage daughters? I've had them — four of them to be exact — so I am a certified professional girl-raiser. There's a phenomenon that usually it hits around 14 (although my youngest got it at 12) where, all of a sudden, instead of Daddy being the apple of their eye, I am now perceived as a nuisance. I'm not relevant, I'm no longer funny, I don't matter. At best, I'm a necessary evil — necessary in the sense that I am good for two things; transportation and compensation...that's it.

Just shut up Dad, don't say anything to my friends and hand over the credit card.. I'm no longer cool, and truly, they begin to wonder if I ever really *was* cool. The less of me the better, just hand over the quid. Welcome, friends, to the world of teenage girls. It's their world, and I don't belong in it. Unless of course, the fat hits the fan, and they *really* need something.

I think that's a pretty good illustration of how we can be with the Almighty. No need to spend time thinking about relationship... this is about results. And really, not much else. But friends, here's the issue: God *is* interested is results, but He's *much* more interested in relationship. *We* want results, *He* wants relationship. It's a problem. Most miss it. And that is why so many get disenchanted with God. They want what they want when they want it...but when whatever they want doesn't happen, then what good was God to them? I love it when someone says, "I tried God, it didn't work." So now God is an "it?" Pretty revealing. But I want to introduce you to the dynamic that needs to be in place. You and I need to focus on our *relationship* with the Lord. As for results and outcomes, we'd best leave that to Him.

Relationship first my friend, then results show up along the way. Simple, but not easy. We would like it the other way around. But man, when I actually get in sync with this and with Him, it is so much better for my mental health. When I focus on spending time with Him (read a Bible, go to a church, talk to a Christian friend or two, read a good book, do wholesome things) and learn to relax and let the results come, it's *such* a better way to live. It takes the pressure off. Allows me to sleep better. Be better. Just works all the way around. And then you and I can just relax, wait, and let His plans unfold.

So, God had a plan for Sarai and Abram. He told them a baby was on the way — but one small detail was left out — He didn't say when! He just said a baby's coming, full stop. Are you not so good with patience? Me neither. Guess what? We learn it. (By being patient.) As much as God does love you and me — and believe it, He does — He doesn't care so much about your timetable. Or mine. It can feel frustrating as hell sometimes ... I don't know how else to put it ... but that's the deal.

So back to my little life, where I'm still waiting to see how it all unfolds. While I *do* feel I'm in the right place, doing the right things, taking the right shots, and making the right moves, I don't know when — or even *if* — it will all work out. And as much as I want to know the answers now (and just so you know, if I do actually hit it out of the park, I'm buying an RV), it's His timing, not mine. But as stated, in the meantime, while I'm waiting for it all to play out, I will listen, I will learn, I will trust, I will focus, and I will grow. I will get better. I will be better. It will be time well spent. Some days I'm good with it. Some days I'm not. But that's the deal, that's how God works.

GET READY

Now when Abram was ninety-nine years old, the LORD appeared to Abram and said to him, "I am God Almighty; Walk before Me, and be blameless. I will make My covenant between Me and you, and I will multiply you exceedingly."

Abram fell on his face, and God talked with him, saying, "As for Me, behold, My covenant is with you, and you will be the father of a multitude of nations. No longer shall you be named Abram, but your name shall be Abraham; for I have made you the father of a multitude of nations."

Then God said to Abraham, "As for your wife Sarai, you shall not call her by the name Sarai, but Sarah shall be her name. I will bless her, and indeed I will give you a son by her. Then I will bless her, and she shall be a mother of nations; kings of peoples will come from her." Then Abraham fell on his face and laughed, and said in his heart, "Will a child be born to a man a hundred years old? And will Sarah, who is ninety years old, give birth to a child? (Genesis 17:1-5, 15-17)

I *so* love this. Easy to love, maybe because it's not my life, but I do love it, nonetheless. Before we get into the meat of it, a couple of things: We just discussed baby #1. Not the baby God promised, but the baby we got when Sarai and Abram called the audible...a baby by another woman. This was not how God drew it up, but what's done is done. Baby on the ground — it's all over. I guess they'll just do the best with what they've got at this point and keep moving. They got the kid by common sense. Go on and make your destiny *your* way. I mean, it's nice to think about, that maybe we could have had a kid together, but it would have been nice if the tooth fairy was really real, too.

Let me share a secret with you.

Sometimes, God's not into common sense.

You get that? You feeling it?

One more time: Sometimes, God is not into common sense! It's easy to just make the best of it and live with the consequences. But 13 years later, here comes the Almighty *yet again* with the same message for Abram: You and your bride — together — are going to make a baby. No third party required. God didn't blink. *They* blinked. So convicting was His message that this time it includes a name change. Abram becomes Abraham which means "Father of Many." In Old Testament times, you were named for what you're like or what you do, so now everybody that sees him coming calls Abram "Father of Many" — Abraham for short.

At 99.

I mean, *beyond* ridiculous.

But that's God.

Not only is Abraham himself older than dirt, bear in mind that Sarah is now a svelte and smooth 90. They have a kid in the house already, but God says, "Remember that promise I made you? We're *still* going to do this! And we're gonna do it *My* way, the way I said it was gonna go down. Because when it's My way, it's the best way, the right way, and guess what? Your age, your impatience, your poor choices, and your weakness won't stop Me.

This script won't change, my plan will move forward, you will be a part of it, and you will like it.

Unbelievable.

So fast forward to like, today. You know how many times I've botched it? Forget *before* I became a Christian and got excited about God — you don't even have the time. Try *afterward*. I'm totally impatient, have quit too early, cut corners, done things my way, shot first/aimed later, put myself first and God second, and basically done almost *everything* Abraham did. Yet, amazingly, incredibly, supernaturally, God still moves with me and through me. He still has plans and a direction for me, still wants me around, still assigns value and purpose to me, and still actually thinks well of me. It is mind boggling to me that God has put up with so much immaturity and self-centeredness on my part (that came easy — I was an only child), but still doesn't give up on me, and will get His money's worth out of me one way or another. *That,* my friend, is huge!

You may know where this is going but let me spell it out for you anyway. That little story and song about God working through Sarah and Abraham's frailties and faults is not reserved just for "special" people. That's your reality as well. Or maybe I need to say it *should* be, and it's *supposed* to be. The simple fact is, when you come to God and seek to get right with Him, then that dynamic becomes your story, too.

Abraham and Sarah — you think they were giants and pillars of strength and faith for God at this point? You know they weren't. Me? Are you kidding? None of us — *none* of us are God's gift to humanity. But in His hands, we can be pretty potent. The point of this rant needs to hit you between the eyes. God doesn't just love, care for, and choose certain people to be with and work through. That's not His way. He loves, cares for, and uses all of us. Believe it! The whole "I'm not worthy" phrase stays with Wayne's World. In *God's* world, you and I *are* worthy. Believe it. Stick a fork in it.

You *are* worthy! Don't you dare chalk this up to churchy, rah-rah, preacher talk. It's as real as you are, sitting here reading this book, so you mark it down. I've never been so serious about anything in my life, so start thinking on this, and we will keep going.

WE MADE IT

The Lord visited Sarah as he had said, and the Lord did to Sarah as he had promised. ² And Sarah conceived and bore Abraham a son in his old age at the time of which God had spoken to him. ³ Abraham called the name of his son who was born to him, whom Sarah bore him, Isaac.

But Sarah saw the son of Hagar the Egyptian, whom she had borne to Abraham, laughing¹⁰ So she said to Abraham, "Cast out this slave woman with her son, for the son of this slave woman shall not be heir with my son Isaac." ¹¹ And the thing was very displeasing to Abraham on account of his son. ¹² But God said to Abraham, "Be not displeased because of the boy and because of your slave woman. Whatever Sarah says to you, do as she tells you, for through Isaac shall your offspring be named. ¹³ And I will make a nation of the son of the slave woman also, because he is your offspring." ¹⁴ So Abraham rose early in the morning and took bread and a skin of water and gave it to Hagar, putting it on her shoulder, along with the child, and sent her away. And she departed and wandered in the wilderness of Beersheba.

15 When the water in the skin was gone, she put the child under one of the bushes. 16 Then she went and sat down opposite him a good way off, about the distance of a bowshot, for she said, "Let me not look on the death of the child." And as she sat opposite him, she lifted up her voice and wept.

Then God opened her eyes, and she saw a well of water. And she went and filled the skin with water and gave the boy a drink. (Genesis 21:1-3, 9-16, 19)

Well, how about *that*? Would you believe, it actually happened? Never thought the day would come, but it did. Sure enough, God comes through. He just delivered; pun intended. Maybe a little later than we'd like — what's a half century among friends — but here we are. We have a baby boy on the ground, just like God said it would be. No adoption, nephew, or kid from down the street. Nope, it's a boy produced right out of a 100-year-old man and his 90-year-old bride. Pretty hilarious, actually. You just have to laugh. Matter of fact, the boy's name was exactly that: Isaac, which means laughter. How appropriate. What else could it be? No way this is real, but it is.

But wait. There is one small problem. There's another boy in the camp — and with him, another mom. Hagar and Ishmael. The brother by a different mother. Remember, God didn't draw it up that way, but that's where we are. Sarah rejects *her own* Plan B — Ishmael — now that God's Plan A has come to pass. Not sure exactly what went down, but we know enough. Sarah has anxiety about Ishmael, and figures there's not enough room for both boys on the ranch. So, she goes to Abraham, unloads on him, tells him to get his son and the *other* mother off the premises.

Old Abraham is in a tight spot. Real tight. You see, even though it was not his idea to have this child, the fact is he *did* have him,

70

and he loves the boy. Has grown close to him. Wants him there as part of the family. But that is most emphatically *not* the opinion of Sarah. There is no love lost between her, the love child, and his mom, so she says they've got to go. Pretty brutal, but that's where it is.

By the way, I told my wife my theory about how Sarah brought all this on herself, and her response was, "It's Abraham's fault."

"What?" I asked, incredulous. "It was *her* idea to have Abraham sleep with Hagar!"

The wife didn't blink. "It's his fault, because he should never have acted on it."

Me: "Un*believ*able."

(The issue is still unresolved.)

But back to it, this thing is raw, the gloves are off, and something's got to give. There are two families in the tent, and no question, that's one too many. Somebody's got to go, and in this case, it's Hagar and Ishmael. No, it's not fair, but that's where this ends up.

So — when you're a single mom on your own in biblical times, that's not good. No husband, no career, no government safety net, no church, and no home for unwed mothers. It's "here's a little food and water for the trip out — good luck." And oh, yeah, they're in the desert. This isn't Laguna Beach. The game is over. It's exit stage left for these two.

But, God's not done.

In the height of depression, when there just is no answer, no way out, nothing left to do — no hope — there is God. Make no mistake, Hagar was planning to die in the desert — the script isn't hard to interpret. She's so despondent and lost that she drops her son off under a bush and walks away. She can't bear to watch him die. Does it get any bleaker than that? But just like with Abraham and Sarah, God has a word for Hagar. Not only are she and her

son going to survive, the boy will *also* be the father of a nation —
a great nation.

This is a red thread that you will see time and time again. Get
used to it. It's big, really big, so don't miss it: Just because you
don't have an answer doesn't mean there isn't one! We've discussed it before, and we'll hit it again. Just because you don't have
an answer doesn't mean there isn't one. This is arguably one of
the greatest truths in the Bible. It's everywhere, in almost every
book, Old Testament, New Testament, doesn't matter. The Bible
is chock full of story after story after story of how God guides
people through ridiculously impossible situations and circumstances. This truth is one of the main reasons why I'm so passionate about my faith, and why I want you to be passionate as
well. God *always* has a plan, a way, an option...even if you and I
don't. That promise and provision is in everything. Say you're
married, and your better half just left the reservation; mentally,
emotionally, physically, *whatever*...God has a plan through that.
Say your health is bad, your finances short, your job awful, your
kids ballistic, your life is just not working out in *any* capacity — I
am here to say, God does lead through *all* that.

Now I have to tell you a story. It's dark, and a lot tragic, but it
applies. It's a week before Christmas a few years ago, just about
the time I'm ready to shut things down for the year and get into
the holiday mode. (Your boy is big on Christmas season: Stay in
pajamas till noon, work out, *don't* work, watch *Christmas Vacation*
and *Lord of the Rings* for the 40th time, smoke turkeys, grill steaks,
drink eggnog, sing carols, love on my kids — whether they like it
or not is irrelevant — in short, enjoy life.) So, I get a call. Said hello,
and immediately I knew something was wrong, like, *bad* wrong.
Some of you have had those calls, right? It was the daughter of
a friend, a fine man, a good man, true family man to the core,
a Christian man. We started a Bible study together in our old

neighborhood, just all of it. Well, the call I got was letting me know that he had just put a gun to his head and pulled the trigger.

What the hell?

Suffice it to say — it wasn't one of my best Christmas seasons, and not a great way to start a New Year. As far as these things go, I guess the story wasn't that unusual. His job of many years had gone away, he tried to do something different, it wasn't working out, and the money was drying up. He was 60ish, and when the strain, the pressure, the weight, the burden of it all became too much, he ended it. Still gets me worked up just writing about it, and it's been a few years now. There was no alcohol or drug addiction, no affairs, no nothing except a complete and total loss of hope.

Folks, whether this hits you hard or whether just reading about Hagar and Ishmael is more than enough for you, the message is crystal clear: God will always have an answer! If all we did was repeat this around 100 times a day for 30 days, it would be time well spent, but regardless, this is one of the greatest messages of the Bible. I take it very literally. When I read and re-read the verses, the stories, the people, and places where there was no hope, the message becomes clear. Time and time again, God is there. He has a way through it. Notice I didn't say all the train wrecks go away, I said He has a way *through* it.

His direction, His leadership, His presence — He doesn't miss. So back to our story. Sure enough, in the middle of the desert, with no water, no food, nowhere to go, no cards left to play, Hagar sees a well. With water. Good water! The kind you drink, and get refreshment from. Won't give you all the details, but Hagar survives, her boy Ishmael survives, and once again we have another story of how God works. By the way, what I'm going to say next is truly deserving of its own book, but I want you to know that sometimes, the good *do* die young. It would be naive and stupid for me to suggest that there are not situations where people die too soon, where people aren't miraculously healed, and where you don't get the great victory story. But here's the trailer: What happens on this side of heaven does not tell the whole story. You see, for those of us who really understand the big picture and who take God and the Bible seriously, whatever happens on this earth is *not* the end game. There is the issue of what happens on the other side, and the teaser is, we who believe in God and His salvation will continue on with Him and there is life after death. That is for another day, but for now, you need to know that the movie doesn't stop when we stop breathing ...not even close.

You *Can't* Be Serious!

Some time later God tested Abraham. He said to him,
"Abraham!"

"Here I am," he replied.

² Then God said, "Take your son, your only son, whom
you love — Isaac — and go to the region of Moriah.
Sacrifice him there as a burnt offering on a mountain
I will show you." (Genesis 22:1-2)

At this point, I'd have only one thing to say if it were me: *No way.* That's it. Two words. *No way.* Okay, maybe three words; no *freaking* way. You are telling me that this couple has been waiting for most of a century to have a baby, finally get one, and then are told to go offer the same baby as a sacrifice...a *sacrifice*? *Animal* sacrifices were given as an offering for sin back in the day...but *not* your own kid! What kind of cruelty is this? This is just *wrong*... and I cannot believe that a loving, caring, kind, wonderful God would ask for that. It defies comprehension, does it not? I mean, let's be Abraham and Sarah for a minute and just vent a little bit; say what any logical person would say.

So God: You call me and my bride out from our household — mind you, we weren't renegades, rebels or malcontents — we were just doing our thing, trying to get by, and then, out of nowhere, for whatever reason, You call *us*. Specifically, You tell us that we're supposed to leave mom and dad, kith and kin, and go to some far off land...never been there, have no *clue* about the place, but regardless, that's the word. So, trying to be upright and obedient, we do it. Yep, we do it. To be fair, you *did* say that we would be a part of something big. Big, like, you're thinking of starting a nation through us, and being that we couldn't have a kid for all our adult lives, that sounds compelling. *Still*, this a big leap of faith. But hey, we're in, and off we go. While wandering and wondering, we don't once jump ship, turn around, and go home. Forget the fact that it took 25 *years* for You to come through for us — and we are becoming parents when we should be *great-grandparents.* That may make things a little challenging, but no matter — we're still in, we're grateful, and it's all good. So now, after a quarter century of waiting for You to come through, just when life with this boy You gave us is getting good, You come up with *this*? *Sacrifice* the boy? Again, you cannot be serious! To be just really blunt, what is Your deal ?

And then:

> *Early the next morning Abraham got up and loaded his donkey. He took with him two of his servants and his son Isaac. When he had cut enough wood for the burnt offering, he set out for the place God had told him about.*[10]

This is one verse that gets its own write up. Just one verse. But it's everything. When you read it, what I want you to notice is what it *doesn't* say. Where is the verbiage that says something like, "Abraham cried out" or "Abraham pleaded with God" or "Abraham fainted" or "Abraham blew up." It's not there. We don't read that Sarah killed herself or Abraham ran away, or said, "No, take me

---

[10] Genesis 22:3

instead," went berserk, had a stroke...*anything* that would seem to be the normal response to this directive. Over the years I've heard sermons, seen incredible artistic renditions of this story that absolutely would depict it as full of horror and gut wrenching, terrifying woe. Honestly, I wonder if you — if you've read this before — have questioned how loving God can be if He would require something like this of His people. I've struggled with it myself. But yet, but *yet* ... look at what this verse actually says. After getting the word from the Almighty about what He wants Abraham to do, what does it say? "Early the next morning Abraham got up and loaded his donkey. He took with him two of his servants and his son Isaac. When he had cut enough wood for the burnt offering, he set out for the place God had told him about."[11] That's *it*? He just goes and *does* it? That response begs the question, *how* could he do that? Has he totally lost it? That's just not right! If I let myself go there, I could question Abraham's mental state. Seriously. Let's face it; the guy's probably around 115 years old at this point — how sharp would *you* be? But that's not it. Abraham was plenty sharp, in his right mind, not drug or alcohol induced ... none of it. You want to know the truth of the matter? I've got it. It's right in front of us. Three words, pure and simple. Here we go:

He was ready.

Yep, that's it. Just one more time to be sure we've got it. Take two:

He was ready.

---

[11] Ibid.

I've read this passage at least 50 times, taught on it, discussed it, thought about it, wondered about it, and only recently did it hit me.

When you are called to leave the safety and security of your homeland and your family to go someplace you've never been before and furthermore, you don't know how long it will take to get there, what you will run into along the way, what you'll do *when* you get there (because deposits of faith are not FDIC insured), when you *do* that — something happens. You change. You grow. You stretch. You get moxie. You start to get strong. To be clear, you don't accomplish all that alone, God accomplishes it through you. But let's keep going.

He and Sarah set out, and Abraham gets a heads up that he's gonna be a dad. Wonderful! A daddy! He's always wanted to be one, and hey, getting that word from the Almighty at the young age of 75 might be considered a bit late by some, but let's not get stuck in the details. A baby's a baby, a family's a family — bring it on! But that's not the whole story. Oh no, we all have to wait an *additional* 25 years to actually birth the boy. What's the point? What's the purpose? Folks, it's all right there. All those years of waiting, wandering, hoping, thinking, praying, laughing, crying, aging, whatever else ... it was all part of the plan. It needed to happen.

You see, if Abraham and Sarah had received God's promises right away — which would have been preferable to them — then you know what? They would *not* have been ready to do what God told them to do with the boy. With everything God had going on with and through them, they would not have been ready! Abraham and Sarah's faith had to be developed, had to be strengthened, man ... and I can tell you from his experience as well as mine that almost every time we are not *born* ready for challenge, we are *made* ready! Abraham had to be made ready with the kind

This story just seems to get more bizarre. All this time, all this waiting for God to deliver, all to have it end like this? But notice something in the fourth and fifth verses: "On the third day Abraham looked up and saw the place in the distance. He said to his servants, 'Stay here with the donkey while I and the boy go over there. We will worship and then we will come back to you.'" Say *what*? Did we get that right? Abraham tells the hired help, "Don't wait up. We'll be back before you know it." Not *I'll* be back, *we'll* be back. Father and son will *both* come back down. Yet, we heard the order from the Almighty Himself: sacrifice the boy. In effect, give him back to Me. So, what did Abraham know? Maybe it gets a little clearer in the eighth verse. When asked by Isaac where the sacrifice was going to come from, Abraham says, "God himself will provide the lamb for the burnt offering."

Hmmm.

Did he say that to placate the kid, or just lie to him and spare him the real answer — maybe keep him from bolting? Possible, but not likely. Was Abraham thinking that Isaac was, in fact, the lamb to be slain, and simply omitting his name when he answered his son? Maybe a little more possible, but still not likely. No, I think the reason Abraham said what he said was because he *knew* that God had something in store for them on that mountain. He *knew* that, after going all this way, going through everything he and Sarah had gone through to get to this place, it wasn't going to end *here*. He knew it! He didn't know how or what exactly was going to happen on that mountain, but he knew, he *knew*, that it would work out.

Welcome to the world of faith. That is what God is looking for. That is how it's supposed to be. When you and I don't know *how* things will work out, but that they *will* work out, then we become players. Then we're for real. We take God at His word. We move forward. We get substance, we gain depth.

There's a whole lot of shallowness in our culture boys and girls, just a whole lot of shallow. Let me share this with you as sweetly as I can: God is not into shallow. What He *is* into is depth, and it took Abraham a quarter of a century-plus to get it, but hey, he did, it's there, and he took off as directed with Isaac to see how this thing was all going to play out. So, here's what I think. Had God told Abraham and Sarah they would have a baby, and then a year later, after their boy is born, commanded them to give him back ...I'm thinking, no way. Abraham *would* have blinked. They wouldn't have been able to do it. Too painful, too valuable, too violating — it's not going to happen. But when you get a promise like they did and then wait 25 years, that's plenty of time to build your faith. Which brings me to my main point:

Faith is built.

I don't believe for one minute that you either have it or you don't.

Faith is *built*.

I absolutely believe that if I continue following God and growing my relationship with Him, I can have more faith a year from now than what I have today. Faith grows. Faith builds. Faith strengthens. So, after living with and trusting God all this time, there is nothing that would derail Abraham. He knows that God *is* in control, He *will* have the last word, He *does* have an answer to every situation — and Abraham was so entrenched in that belief that when he got the word to take Isaac up the mountain, he just did it.

Genesis 22: 11-18

¹¹ *But the angel of the* L<small>ORD</small> *called out to him from heaven, "Abraham! Abraham!"*

"Here I am," he replied.

¹² *"Do not lay a hand on the boy," he said. "Do not do anything to him. Now I know that you fear God, because you have not withheld from me your son, your only son."*

¹³ *Abraham looked up and there in a thicket he saw a ram caught by its horns. He went over and took the ram and sacrificed it as a burnt offering instead of his son.* ¹⁴ *So Abraham called that place The* L<small>ORD</small> *Will Provide. And to this day it is said, "On the mountain of the* L<small>ORD</small> *it will be provided."*

¹⁵ *The angel of the* L<small>ORD</small> *called to Abraham from heaven a second time* ¹⁶ *and said, "I swear by myself, declares the* L<small>ORD</small>*, that because you have done this and have not withheld your son, your only son,* ¹⁷ *I will surely bless you and make your descendants as numerous as the stars in the sky and as the sand on the seashore. Your descendants will take possession of the cities of their enemies,* ¹⁸ *and through your offspring all nations on earth will be blessed, because you have obeyed me."*

BALL GAME

This thing is over. Stick a fork in it. Sure enough, baby boy doesn't die. Another sacrifice is found. All is well. God is indeed good. This really isn't so much about God as it is Abraham. You see — I've learned a few things in my little life, and one of them is, God will move in me to the extent that I respond. I need to show up, and God will guide it from there. Sometimes I need to show up and *keep* showing up, and let God move with me and through me as He sees fit. Most of the time I'm good with that — no doubt I can get upside down waiting on things to transpire — but I've seen the pattern enough to know that if I keep coming to God, God will come through for me. Probably not on *my* timetable, and probably not the way I'd script it, but it doesn't matter, God comes through. While I admit the timetable part is a bear, at least I know, I *know*, that the waiting time is building time — and I'm getting better and better with that.

About the scripting I mentioned ... this is a big one. I think you understand that life throws curve balls, yes? You know this, right? You get that there are things that happen to us that we can't control, can't influence, and don't understand. In Abraham's case, I *guarantee* he didn't see that part of the scripting would be to sacrifice his son. No way. I also guarantee that the news probably popped him pretty good. But yet, as discussed ad nauseum, he *goes*. He does his part. He shows up. That's big-time faith. That's rhino-sized trust. That's just huge. And that's really what God wants from us. Show up. Trust. Have faith that God's got this, whatever the "this" is. When that happens, everything moves forward.

You know what I think? If Abraham blinked, if he stuttered, quit, told God "It ain't happening," went the other way, said, "I'm outta here," God would have kept moving. He has a plan. But Abraham would not have been a part of it. At least not the part that God *wanted* him to play. That's not punishment. That's not being vindictive. It's about doing the best we know how, as God would have us do. And keep going. Just *keep going*. This whole episode is about that. God laid it out there, told Abraham what to do, and Abraham had the faith, had the spiritual *guts* to move forward, to keep going.

Maybe you think it's bad that God would test them like that, but when you're going to build an entire nation and rewrite history with a couple, you gotta know they have the right stuff in them to make it work. I've lived a lot of my life *not* showing up. I can't go back and re-live it, and that's disappointing — but I darn sure can do all I can to keep going now. That's all he wants from us, bro. We keep going.

What happened to Abraham *after* he and Isaac came back down the mountain? After Abraham passed the impossible test? Well, "Then Abraham returned to his servants, and they set off together for Beersheba. And Abraham stayed in Beersheba."[12] *That's it*? I don't know if it hits you like it did me, but I found it rather shocking that all this sacrifice-your-son drama just seemed to *end*. It was just *over*. I mean, everybody just goes back down the mountain and goes home. We're done here. Move on. You'd think there'd be room for, I don't know, a celebration? How about a nice feast, maybe bring in some quality BBQ, bring some folks in from out of town and just have a whale of a weekend. Or maybe an honor or two, perhaps an accolade for the old man

---

[12] Genesis 22:19

85

somewhere in here? If it were me, I'm thinking I make a request — you know, get a little something for the effort. Ask the Almighty like, say, "How about making me a king? Or at *least* give me a feature story on "How I Did It," with a made-for-TV-movie to follow?"

Nope. None of that. You know what I think? Because Abraham was so built up with faith, so full of confidence in God's providence, the whole episode was just not that big a deal to him. He really knew that somehow God had His hands all over this, that He had a reason and an answer for this whole situation, and after it was all said and done, he could just go back down the mountain and let that be that.

DUCKS IN A ROW

Abraham was now very old, and the Lord had blessed him in every way. ²He said to the senior servant in his household, the one in charge of all that he had, "Put your hand under my thigh. ³I want you to swear by the Lord, the God of heaven and the God of earth, that you will not get a wife for my son from the daughters of the Canaanites, among whom I am living, ⁴but will go to my country and my own relatives and get a wife for my son Isaac." (Genesis 24:1-4)

So, here's progress. To make sure you understand, Abraham is in his last days. His time is about up. But he wants to do a couple more things; namely, he wants to get his house in order. By the way, one indication that the Almighty is working in your life is that you want to get your house in order. You want to get your mind right, your surroundings right, your lifestyle right, your money right, your relationships right, your priorities right ... just all of it.

So, for Abraham, part of the plan is that God's promise keeps going. And for that to happen, his boy Isaac needs to find a wife. But not just any woman, any companion, any wife. This woman will be part of the plan — God's plan. The master plan. You know what's really important to note here? Abraham knows he is a part of something bigger than himself. He knows that what is going on is emphatically *not* all about him. He's a part of something way bigger, and he knows he still has a role to play.

You know why that's a big deal? Because that's what living for God is all about. Let me explain. I was not put on this planet just to grow up, get a job, get married, produce offspring, play tennis, smoke BBQ, watch football, go fishing (with a guide of course, I pay full retail), and die. That is *so* off. When you and I get right with God, we get purpose. When we align ourselves with Him, things *happen*. We become a part of something way bigger than just the day-to-day. Oh yeah, *way* bigger. And you know what else? It doesn't stop. Oh no, baby — it does not stop. Ever!

Not long ago I had the opportunity to do something I've never done before. Specifically, I was a speaker at a Christian conference. But this was no ordinary conference. I've spoken to youth groups, married groups, singles groups, women's groups, men's groups ... but this one was a bit out of the box. Namely, I was speaking at a Senior Living Community. I'm betting the average age was at least 86. Anyway, you know who put it on? The people who lived there! The residents themselves! Not the staff, not the activities director, the *residents*! It wasn't just me; they brought in another speaker from out of state, set it all up, coordinated it, and sure enough, the people came.

The message in this story is that, while being with them those few days, I learned a valuable truth: you don't retire. Ever! We're not built for it. These folks came because they wanted to hear a word. They wanted some encouragement and reinforcement that God wasn't done with them yet, and man, I will tell you He's not done with *any* of us as long as we're on this side of heaven. We all need a hill to climb, something to work on, a path to follow. You say you don't have any purpose right now? Trust me, get right with God and you will.

I presided over a funeral the other day.

The guy we buried, honored, and remembered worked until he was 82. His kids told me he lamented that he didn't do more. Billy Graham — ever heard of him? Billy preached his last public message at 97. *What?* That's right, 97. Graduated and went to the Kingdom at 99. What a player! But that shouldn't be just for him. That's for all of us. A purpose is where it's at, man. We may think it's all about pleasure, but that's a head fake. Purpose *begats* pleasure. The more purpose we have, the more pleasure we get.

Personally, the idea of living for the pension so you can get up, have breakfast, read the paper, transition to the couch, sleep, get up, eat lunch, sleep again, watch the news and putz away the rest of the day only to do it again tomorrow, leaves a lot on the table. If that's your end game, then maybe living with and for God isn't for you. But if you've read this far, my sense is that you have at least some desire to see what God has for you, and if He can fill your life and make it sizzle. With probably a few hundred million people joining me as witnesses over the ages, I can say that God *does* have a plan in place, and He would very much like you to participate with Him in it. In God's program, you and I always have a reason to get up in the morning.

It's Gotta Be Right

² He said to the senior servant in his household, the one in charge of all that he had, "Put your hand under my thigh. ³ I want you to swear by the LORD, the God of heaven and the God of earth, that you will not get a wife for my son from the daughters of the Canaanites, among whom I am living, ⁴ but will go to my country and my own relatives and get a wife for my son Isaac."

⁵ The servant asked him, "What if the woman is unwilling to come back with me to this land? Shall I then take your son back to the country you came from?"

⁶ "Make sure that you do not take my son back there," Abraham said. ⁷ "The LORD, the God of heaven, who brought me out of my father's household and my native land and who spoke to me and promised me on oath, saying, 'To your offspring[a] I will give this land' — he will send his angel before you so that you can get a wife for my son from there. (Genesis 24:2-7)

Time flies , doesn't it ? Abraham knows that Isaac needs to marry and needs to marry a woman from the family — namely the family from which God called Abraham. Isaac wasn't meant to marry just anyone — stay on point here — his wife needs to be from the same heritage, from the place Abraham came from. So, the message is really clear to number one servant: You go, take Isaac with you, get back to the motherland, and get a girl for him. The show goes on. You see, when God works, it's rarely random. In this case, at this point in time, God used a specific family to initiate His plan. Today, it's not about a family, a race, or even a nation God has selected, but his actions are planned. Personally, I'm good with that. I like that I have a sovereign God in place who knows more than I do, sees more than I see, and has a destiny for me that I want to be a part of.

One quick comment — you've got to be on board with what I'm going to say here — whatever you want out of life going forward, you've got to want what God wants *more* than what you want. One more time: Whatever you want out of life, you've got to want what God wants for you *more* than what you want. That's how this works, compadre. Why exactly would you do that? Well, here's the deal: Whatever God has in store for you as we all move forward...*whatever* that is (and you may be completely clueless about it at this point), you've got to be willing to say that He knows more than you know, He sees more than you see, and because He's Almighty God, He will have a better plan and purpose than we could construct ourselves.

Oh, don't get me wrong — you may be able to accomplish quite a lot for yourself just doing it all by your lonesome; plenty of people that probably couldn't care less about God are proof positive of that. But there's a whole lot more at stake here than how rich, famous, successful, or good looking you get. This has everything to do with total quality of life, and that includes a whole lot of things over and above the material. So, my motivation for putting God front and center in my life is that He can maximize whatever potential, gifts, aptitudes, and talents are out there much better than I can. My experience, my hope, my trust, is that He can do a much better job of building the right stuff in me than me than I can by going solo. That's it.

Just so you know, I can come up with all kinds of ideas as to what would bring me the best bang for my buck in this little life of mine. All kinds of ideas. How about getting financially set, just knock a career out of the park, live in certain places — or at least hang out in them — have really cool hobbies, wear the right clothes, take the cool trips, even fight for the right causes. And there's nothing wrong with any of that. But here's the deal: if God is not in and through and under all that, then something is not going to be quite right. Something's gonna be missing, something's a bit off. Maybe not immediately, but at some juncture, we'll just sense it, or maybe feel it. So in summary, what I've learned and what I continue to learn (because the learning never stops with Him) is that the more rightly related to God I am, the more aligned I am with what He wants, the better I am, and the better my life is. It doesn't mean that everything else just falls into place, but man, we are much more in tune and on point *with* Him than without Him.

JUST DOIN' MY JOB

⁸ If the woman is unwilling to come back with you, then you will be released from this oath of mine. Only do not take my son back there." ⁹ So the servant put his hand under the thigh of his master Abraham and swore an oath to him concerning this matter.

¹⁰ Then the servant left, taking with him ten of his master's camels loaded with all kinds of good things from his master. He set out for Aram Naharaim[a] and made his way to the town of Nahor. (Genesis 24:8-10)

J ust three little verses here, they don't get a lot of press, not the most exciting passage you've ever read, but regardless, there's some big stuff here. Big stuff!

We're talking here about Abraham's servant. The would-be matchmaker. Abraham gives him a job, more like a mission in military jargon. What we have here is not exactly standard work for the hired help; this is not an ordinary run of the mill task.

Abraham: Go find my kid a wife.

Servant: Sure. Anything else, boss? Height? Weight? Brown eyes or blue? Seriously? Who does that? Granted, back in the day you had arranged marriages, but this was different...this old boy didn't even *know* these people. I mean, what's the pitch gonna be? "Hi, you don't know me, but I work for one of your long-lost kin. It's been a while — oh, maybe 40 years or so, but hey, they had a son awhile back, a baby boy when Sarah was about 90. It's a little crazy, I know — but anyway, the kid is now about marrying age and, well, they didn't want him to marry just *anybody*. No, you see, they're beyond convinced it needs to be somebody from their own bloodline, and well, the word is, on this side of the desert, *you're it*.

So, uhm, if any of you have any single women running around that don't seem too fired up with what they're working with locally, well, we may have another option for them.

Uh, no, he's not here, and there are no pictures. They live a long way from here so you might not ever see your girl again — but aside from all that, it might work out. She could really be happy I think, and the benefits are great because his dad is rich.

I mean, what else can the guy say? How do you pull this off? Herding camels is one thing. This? Not so much.

But wait a minute. There's a clause. A huge, game changing clause. I want you to re-read verse 8: "*If the woman is unwilling to come back with you, then you will be released from this oath of mine...*".

I'm so glad that came out. Because there's a lesson here, a lesson just as relevant today as it was back then. Very simply, when we're about the work of the Lord, our number one job is to show up. Did you get that? Show up! Let God handle some of the finer points, sure, but one more time, our part is to just show up. Participate! And then, when you do, you'll probably get a read on what's next.

So let me share this little pearl of wisdom: the spiritual, emotional, and mental health of the human race would take a quantum leap forward if we realized that living life for God really is about doing what we're called to do, led to do, and then leaving the results entirely to Him. Where it all ends up, we may not know, but if we're in the lane we're supposed to be in, life flows a whole lot better.

I'll give you an example. Me and my business partner — we're building this thing, a thing that hasn't really been done in our industry. We think we're on to something here, hoping this idea works, but as said before, we don't know for sure. We are climbing the hills, we are on the phones, in the planes, on the road, living in hotels, kissing babies, hugging their mothers, and even their dads if we have to. With this particular venture, we're almost five years into it, but the simple fact is, there's not a whole lot we can control with this thing. To make sure you get it, there is absolutely no guarantee we're going to pop it. To be really blunt, it might not work at all! That is Truth #1. And Truth #2? We'll do our work and leave the results to God.

I can tell you that as of this day, date, and time, I feel led to go the direction we're going. I'm staying in my lane. If it works, that's really cool, but if it doesn't, I will have done the best I could do, and whatever the result, I can live with it. I'll show up and rely on God to do the rest. And if the verse we read is any indicator, we will be good with whatever happens. It's the doing, not so much the accomplishing that wins the war. Abraham told his servant, just do what I ask you to do. And the servant did.

Whether or not you get the results you hoped for, whatever the deal, if you made the appearance and took your cut at the ball —- then we take our props from that. We can feel good about that. That is mental health. That is peace. And if somebody else doesn't like it, you don't give a rip. You and God make the plan, and we'll live with what we get.

STICK A FORK IN IT

*Then he prayed, "L*ORD*, God of my master Abraham, make me successful today, and show kindness to my master Abraham. ¹³ See, I am standing beside this spring, and the daughters of the townspeople are coming out to draw water. ¹⁴ May it be that when I say to a young woman, 'Please let down your jar that I may have a drink,' and she says, 'Drink, and I'll water your camels too'—let her be the one you have chosen for your servant Isaac. By this I will know that you have shown kindness to my master."*

¹⁵ Before he had finished praying, Rebekah came out with her jar on her shoulder. She was the daughter of Bethuel son of Milkah, who was the wife of Abraham's brother Nahor.

¹⁷ The servant hurried to meet her and said, "Please give me a little water from your jar."

¹⁸ "Drink, my lord," she said, and quickly lowered the jar to her hands and gave him a drink.

> [19] *After she had given him a drink, she said, "I'll draw water for your camels too, until they have had enough to drink." (Genesis 24:12-15, 17-19)*

This baby's over. Just over! Notice the phrase in verse 15, "Before he had finished praying..." God was just in it, was He not? I mean, this old boy didn't even finish out his prayer for God's sake, and here comes Miss Wonderful. I'm gonna beat this horse one more time, but it's worth doing it; the servant didn't do anything except to do his part! He just ran the traps, and my oh my, look what happened! I guarantee you he didn't have great wisdom, incredible insight, wasn't clairvoyant, didn't hypnotize anyone, and was not some master dealmaker. No, rather, he did his job the best he could, threw it out there, and God was in it.

I love it when it works that way! The servant gets props because he did what he was supposed to do. We get our props when we do our part. So, what you and I need to be about is getting prayed up, taking the first step, then the next, then the next, then the next. Once a door gets shut, we bounce off it and keep going. Another shuts, the same thing. When God's in it, we just say that God's got another door, another room, maybe another hotel, even another street — doesn't matter. We put God in front of it, we take our swings, we keep moving, and see where it leads.

And by the way, while we're on the subject of work, there's a good word in the other half of the Bible (the New Testament), about how we're supposed to go about our business. The admonition is, "Work hard and cheerfully at all you do, just as though you were working for the Lord..."[13] That's another pearl of truth. The old adage, "Go to work and then you die" ... you don't get that in the Bible. Oh no, the mandate from the Almighty is, you go to work, and you *like* it. You like it because it's part of good, godly

---

[13] Colossians 3:23

living. It's bigger than the boss, the paycheck, the commute, and the software. I'm telling you, when we follow His plan and His lead, that stuff will work itself out. You just keep going, you keep praying, and God keeps moving.

If you went to work, gave it your best, stayed cheerful as best you knew how — just because God said to — then you came home and were basically pleasant...guess what *jefe*? You had yourself a good day. Whatever the markets, customers, partners, bosses, weather, or technology did or didn't do to cooperate, well, I care, but I don't care. We have a different standard. We gage our performance on how much we tried, did what we knew to do, and kept going. You show up, you work hard, you like it, and you leave it in God's hands. That's the best therapy there could be. That is how we should gage a day. This servant was not a superhero, he was just a man who did his part, and relied on God to do rest. I may make a billion bucks one day or I may not, but it doesn't really matter. What matters is that I want the absolute best out of life, and I want that God's way.

So back to the story, would you believe the servant gets his girl? That's right —Rebekah enters the scene, she buys into the plan, she feels led to go marry a guy she's never met (and to be sure, you understand, she *did* have a say), and God's plan to build out his people through the bloodline of Abraham is still on track.

Deja Vu

¹⁹ *This is the account of the family line of Abraham's son Isaac.*

Abraham became the father of Isaac, ²⁰ *and Isaac was forty years old when he married Rebekah daughter of Bethuel the Aramean from Paddan Aram and sister of Laban the Aramean.*

²¹ *Isaac prayed to the LORD on behalf of his wife, because she was childless. The LORD answered his prayer, and his wife Rebekah became pregnant.* ²² *The babies jostled each other within her, and she said, "Why is this happening to me?" So she went to inquire of the LORD.*

²³ *The LORD said to her,*

"Two   nations   are   in   your   womb,
  and two peoples from within you will be separated;
one people will be stronger than the other,
  and the older will serve the younger."

²⁴ *When the time came for her to give birth, there were twin boys in her womb.* ²⁵ *The first to come out was red, and his whole body was like a hairy garment; so they*

named him Esau[26] *After this, his brother came out,
with his hand grasping Esau's heel; so he was named
Jacob. Isaac was sixty years old when Rebekah gave
birth to them. (Genesis 25: 19-26)*

So here we go.

Again.

Isaac and Rebekah. It's their turn to take center stage, have kids, and continue God's ultimate plan to create a people He will use who are dedicated to Him. This marriage took place a little later for Isaac — he's 40; Rebekah's younger. But regardless, they need to have some kids right about now. Trying hard, but no luck. We're not going to do *this* again, are we? From the time of wanting kids to having them, we're talking 20 years for these two. When Isaac's mom and dad got the word, they would have *one* kid, it was 25 years before he arrived. (Can't this ever just happen in, like, nine months?) Do you see a pattern here? Twenty-five years, and then twenty years?

Have you ever had to wait for something in your little life, or is it just me? Just like his parents, Isaac has to wait. But we can't leave it there. If the wait is a part of it, then we have to find *value* in it...we have to see *purpose* in the wait. We won't go through it all again, but what we will review is — just like mom and dad — Isaac and Rebekah needed to grow strong, be built, get prepared, so that they could fulfill their roles and do their part. Again, the wait is just a part of it my friends. But remember, waiting is not wasting. Waiting is building. Take heart, baby: whatever you're waiting on, in God's hands, things are happening. If God wants that thing, you're waiting on to happen, then it will. On His time. If He's *not* in it, you're better off without it. It's that simple. There's a lot to be learned in the wait, so keep yourself together. God's got you, and God's got this. Just. Keep. Going.

So now, with Isaac and Rebekah, we're going to see another pattern. It's the pattern of inconsistency, of upside down, of "how it's *not* supposed to work," or maybe just the pattern of "that makes *no* sense." Get used to it because we're gonna see that pattern a *lot.* You could make the case that we've seen it already, like when people old enough to be grandparents and great grandparents are having newborns, but regardless, we don't want to miss this. So, when Rebekah gets pregnant, she does it well. Turns out she has not one, but two buns in the oven. Not only that, but the twins also seem to be getting rough in there — lots of pushing and shoving going on. (That's putting it mildly; she's probably getting her insides kicked out.) She naturally wonders what this is all about, so she does what all of us should do when we don't understand things: she goes to "inquire of the Lord."

A teaching moment here. Do you ever "inquire of the Lord?" You ever actually ask Him to weigh in on your situation, get involved in your day to day, your plans, your issues? Do you even realize that God *wants* to be engaged in your life and mine — every aspect of it — that He wants us to reach out, ask, inquire, bring Him in and confer? If you don't, you need to get that right. Today. God *wants* to be in your life. So Rebekah doesn't know what's going on inside of her, and when she asks God about it, His response was way bigger than what she was looking for. God in effect says, "You got two boys in there. They both will lead a nation — different nations to be sure — but here's the kicker: the older one will serve the younger one. The leadership and legacy of God's people will come through the second-born son, not the first."

That's unusual — actually it's flat out backward, not the standard protocol, and just not the way it's supposed to be. For some context, you have to understand that in Old Testament times, the first born gets everything. He's the one that takes over the family business. He's the one that gets most of the wealth when dad's gone, the one that will assume the leadership of the family. And if there's a nation of destiny to come out of this family, it will be from son #1. Sons or daughters from #2 on down don't get the blessings that #1 gets. Doesn't work that way. There's no debate about this. It's just the way things are.

Let me share a little secret with you.

God is not interested in "the way things are."

Nope.

He doesn't operate in a box. God is God, and God operates the way He wants. The old prophet Isaiah said, "His ways are not our ways," and boy, you'd best believe it. And you know what? I, for one, am grateful for it. I am glad God works the way God works. I am glad that life is not always cut and dried. You and I know that some wild stuff goes on around here, but the simple fact is, we need that sense of the unknown, that sense of adventure, in living a life that challenges "the way things are." God doesn't operate to code. There are all kind of things that we can experience in living for Him. I want a God who is not limited by the conventional but can interject surprise, wonder, and amazement into the whole thing. I *want* that. (At least most of the time.)

I come from a single parent situation. Not ideal, not how it was supposed to work, but guess what? In God's hands, that's not going to keep me from having the best life possible. I'm not limited by it. I didn't go to a big-time university, didn't come from money, prestige, or privilege, didn't do so hot on the SAT, ACT, or any other tests they threw out there. I'm not particularly well rounded; couldn't tell you how to hold a hammer or anything else that would be classified as a tool (and by the way, I don't *care* ... either my wife fixes it, or I hire professionals). I'm bad with technology, was a crappy college basketball player, and to top it all off, I'm incredibly near sighted. But it doesn't matter. God just blows all that up. If He wants you or me to lead a nation, trust me, we'll lead a nation.

So, to be clear, it doesn't matter if you're the youngest, oldest, plumpest, skinniest, tallest, shortest, plainest, cutest, richest, or poorest person you know. In the hands of the living God, you matter. Everybody matters. Everybody is fair game for His glory, and you will see this time and time again. God's got a plan, a master plan, and if He decides that part of that master plan is for the younger son to carry the torch rather than the older, that's all good, baby, that's just all good.

My parting comment on the subject is, if the human race really understood how much value God places on each of us, over half of our problems as a society would be gone. It's a topic for another day, but it's the truth.

THE HARDER WAY

Now there was a famine in the land—besides the previous famine in Abraham's time—and Isaac went to Abimelek king of the Philistines in Gerar. ² The LORD appeared to Isaac and said, "Do not go down to Egypt; live in the land where I tell you to live. ³ Stay in this land for a while, and I will be with you and will bless you. For to you and your descendants I will give all these lands and will confirm the oath I swore to your father Abraham. ⁴ I will make your descendants as numerous as the stars in the sky and will give them all these lands, and through your offspring all nations on earth will be blessed,⁵ because Abraham obeyed me and did everything I required of him, keeping my commands, my decrees and my instructions." ⁶ So Isaac stayed in Gerar. (Genesis 26:1-6)

S o here's the family of Isaac, just trying to get by, trying to do the right things, make right decisions. But we have a problem. A significant problem. There's nothing to eat, maybe even nothing to drink. There's a famine, and nobody likes those. I don't remember where I read it, but word is, when they have famines in the desert, they do it right. First off, only certain places can even grow food, and when those go down for lack of water, everything goes ... plants, animals, all of it. So, there in the middle of the desert, Isaac and company are thinking it's time to go. Thinking, maybe, Egypt. They at least have the Nile River, and that's better than nothing. It makes all the sense in the world, right?

One small issue.

God's not into moving to Egypt.

But wait — there's food and water in Egypt. There's relief in Egypt. Anything has to be better than where they're at now, right? Come on, people — this place is *done*. We need to leave, because you *know* the palm trees in Egypt are absolutely greener than they are here. Making this move out of here just makes sense.

Unless God's not in it.

So, here's a story that's a little more current. I'd moved to Houston for a job, met and married the lovely wife, and about a year into this thing, she shows up pregnant. Unplanned, unprepared, but it's game on, we're in. Living in the classic 2-bedroom/2- bath starter apartment and obviously adding personnel to the family, so it's time to move from starter apartment to starter home. It all works. Then two more offspring hit the ground. We're popping kids out at a nice clip. Need to expand yet again. More square footage is optimal. Side bar here: just so you know, it was *never* a life-long dream of mine to live in the resort city of Houston. To be honest, Houston probably would have been 8th or 9th out of a list of 12 if I had to rank it. It's hot, it's humid, no family nearby, two friends, lousy traffic, and organically grown mosquitos so big in the summer you grill them. Regardless, that's where the job was, so that's where I went.

But when we are looking for the bigger place yet again, the thought hit me, and man, it was *huge*. Go home. Return to the land of your birth. Go back to your place of origin. The motherland. Austin. Wow — what a revelation. It was mind blowing. I mean, what's not to like about Austin? All my family was there: aunts, uncles, cousins, grandad (the same one that told me to join the Marines — but I loved him anyway), my saintly mother even. It's all good! And then, to make it better, friends, college buddies,

Hill Country, lakes, things to do, and traffic that's at least toler-able. So I go to my company, say I want to relocate, and they say it's all good, we're happy if you're happy. Sold the wife, she's on board, tell mom I'm on my way — she's ecstatic, my kids are too young to care. Seriously could this line up any better? It's the Texas version of Return *of the Native*. It was my destiny — all meant to be. Until it wasn't.

It just wasn't.

We went up there, looked at homes, looked at neighborhoods, wanted the feel, wanted the vibe ... and there wasn't any. Just no mojo. So, we did it again. And again. No pulse on this thing. Mind you, nothing *happened* per se, no torpedo sunk the ship, no dra-matic calamity, no drama, no trauma. But there just weren't any sparks flying. No chemistry.

Have you ever really wanted to date someone; everything seemed like it should line up, like they would be the perfect match, and when you finally had the date, well, it was anti-climactic? Just a dead cat bounce, you know? It was like that. I remember driving back to Houston with the wife riding shotgun, kids strapped in the back. I'm thinking, "I've just sold the world on coming to Austin, and the overwhelming feeling is — it ain't Austin." So, fig-uring I'd be backhanded on the Interstate but wanting to get it over with, I just looked over and told the wife: "God's not in this."

She looked back at me and said: "I know." There it was.

The closer we got to the move, the more we both knew that no matter how good it smelled, sounded, and looked on paper — God wasn't in it. So, you know what? It didn't happen. We stayed in Houston. Been here ever since. Grilled more mosquitoes, sat in Houston traffic with half a million of my closest friends on a daily basis, and we carried on. Oh, don't think I didn't try again. In over 30 years of living here, we tried moving to Austin once, a suburb of Houston twice, a *different* suburb of Houston twice, and yet a third suburb once (Houston is surrounded by suburbs ...they pop up like daisies down here). On one of those expeditions, I actually bought some property in a development that was destined for success and ended up having to sell it ... at a loss. Probably the only guy in Southeast Texas to lose on that deal.

What's the point in all this? I have learned from experience that when we surrender to God and say we want him in our lives, He takes that really seriously. And folks, that gets into the details. As stated, you and I may not spawn a nation or develop bitcoin (is it even real?), but make no mistake, when we live for God there is a plan in place. And take it from one who knows — that's a good thing! I *want* that plan, I *want* that leadership, I want that sense of purpose, that feeling that I'm where I'm supposed to be, doing what I'm supposed to be doing. I want God active and moving in my life, and if that means I stay in the same hot and humid city in the same hot and humid neighborhood working in the same hot and humid job, then I'm good with it. Matter of fact, I embrace it! I don't have to go to Egypt. Or Austin. Or anywhere else. If — and only if — God says go, I go. If He says stay, I stay. Once more, for about the tenth time, if my most important goal in this life is to stay rightly related to God Almighty, then where I live, who I marry, how many kids I have, what kind of money I make, what job I do, what hobbies I have, where I vacation and what I accomplish ... all that flows from my relationship with Him. Trust me, the rest of life will find it's place.

Life may be hard ... It may be real hard, but if God's in it, it will be worthwhile. That's the deal. This isn't all about a prosperity ride. But it *is* about a worthwhile ride, and that's the one we want. So, Isaac and Rebekah, they get kudos on this one. Egypt looked great, nice, and wonderful — right up there with Austin — but they stayed on point. Good for them.

THE PAYOFF

12 Isaac planted crops in that land and the same year reaped a hundredfold, because the LORD blessed him. 13 The man became rich, and his wealth continued to grow until he became very wealthy. 14 He had so many flocks and herds and servants that the Philistines envied him. 15 So all the wells that his father's servants had dug in the time of his father Abraham, the Philistines stopped up, filling them with earth.

16 Then Abimelek said to Isaac, "Move away from us; you have become too powerful for us."

17 So Isaac moved away from there and encamped in the Valley of Gerar, where he settled. (Genesis 26:12-17)

Here's a bit of a follow up, but it's an important follow up. We know that Isaac wanted to make a move, but God said no, so Isaac stayed put. And look what happened. This passage, like many in the Old Testament, describes God's blessing of Isaac in very material terms. Namely, the crops he planted just exploded. Went viral. A hundred-fold is what the Bible says. Let's figure it this way: every dollar he invested is now worth $100.00. If he put $10,000 in the ground, it grew (pun intended) to a cool million. In one year. *Nice.* Apparently, this went on for a while. Isaac and Rebekah got seriously rich. Adult-money rich. He diversified, got into the sheep and goat business, and hit it out of the park again. Our boy is just killing it. In fact, if it's possible, he almost gets *too* rich. This hacks off the neighbors, so much so that they invite him to leave. I think the implication is, "At the rate you're going, you're gonna get into the acquisition business, and we're not really looking to be acquired ... so why don't you take your show and plant it somewhere else?" So, Isaac and Rebekah move.

There's a number of things going on here, but I want to focus on this: when we are aligned with God's plan, following God's direction for our lives ... when we are where He wants us to be, doing what He wants us to do and living the way He wants us to live ... then my friends, *life tends to get good.* You think all this happens if they had jumped ship and gone to Egypt? Doubtful. Certainly, they could have been given a second chance, but had they bolted, things would have been different. They might have gotten some initial relief from the famine, but then that's it. We'll never know of course, but quite possibly it could have gotten worse for them. In Egypt they'd be considered refugees for sure, and I'm not familiar with many refugee success stories in the Old Testament. Not the kind where financial dreams come true, at least in a legal line of work. But because Isaac and Rebekah stayed the course, didn't flinch (at least not much), and stayed where they were supposed to — even though it didn't look great at the time — they did well. Turns out, really well.

You need to understand; Isaac and Rebekah's story is not unusual. When we're on track with God, good things happen. Man, if people just believed that! It's not about all the material wealth, it's that we are in sync with where God has us, and that is where we want to be. So, feeling good, feeling right, having life *flow* ... that's supposed to happen. It's how things work in God's economy. That's kingdom living.

Before we go any further, let's get one thing right — and that's how to interpret God's blessing, God's favor. I don't know about you, but it gets me going when I see some overblown, charismatic, bouffant-haired, polyester pastor and their wonderful wife with even bigger hair claiming God's riches are just around the corner for you and me if we pray long enough, loud enough, and hard enough. And oh yeah, we gotta *give* enough as well — throw that in the cocktail, too. It just blows my mind: "Ohhh saints, just pray and give like there's no tomorrow, then back that truck up and load up all the blessings ... a hundredfold for everybody! Abundance is just waiting for you sweetheart — come on down, 'cause the price is indeed right...woohoo!"

What a crock.

Let me tell you about God's favor, God's blessing, God's peace, God's joy. While there are many examples in the Bible of God bestowing material benefits on His people, that is *not* the only way we determine whether God has blessed us. Far from it. If that were true, then why aren't the missionaries in Africa all driving Porsches? How about those in China? They got second homes waiting for them in Scottsdale? What about inner-city pastors? Are they bringing in a million a year with full benefits? What about them? Where's the bling for all those who love God and serve Him?

Let me tell you where God's riches are *really* found.

They're in the heart.

In the soul.

In the mind.

That's the deal. It is that sense of peace, of purpose, of well-being, of gratitude, of centeredness, of being in your lane, doing what you're supposed to be doing, that fulfills. That is the deal. Oh, don't get me wrong. Those living with and for God can absolutely receive material benefits, but that is not the measuring stick by which we determine the extent of God's blessing in our lives.

I need you to go deep with me here for a minute, so hang on and just be open. For those of us in the West — as in Western civilization — material abundance is everything. Everything. And that includes many in the Western church. Prosperity sells sweetheart, and all over our world we are hit with it. From the earliest age we are told to study hard, work hard, play hard, pray hard, and there *will* be a pot of gold for us at the end of the journey. I've lived by that creed for most of my life, and I bet some of you have as well. Just now, just *now*, after 32 years of living as a believer, I think I am starting to unwind from that. I *think* I am getting to a place where wealth and success in and of themselves are not going to define me. As I've stated, I want to hit it, and hit it hard in my business pursuits, but thinking that I'll get close to God so that I can grab the golden ring of material success is not what the end game with God is supposed to be. We have made that the end-all to be-all, not God. I want to do well in whatever I put my mind to, but I've got to get the place where I do my best for the love of the game, *His* game, and what I'm really after is God's peace and presence in my life, not the big house, car, or bank account.

Why all the verbiage on this? Because we probably lose more people to the faith when all they read, see, and hear from the stage and pulpit is how great things are gonna be materially if you throw your lot in with God. That's just bad theology, man. You and I can expect God to meet our needs, but the real riches, the real joy, the real peace comes from having Him in the center of our lives. If you're like me, there's a whole lot of cleansing and purging we have to go through to get to that place, but it's worth the ride.

The sad thing about this for me is that by the time I knock it through the uprights businesswise, I will have been so weaned off the pursuit of riches I'll end up just figuring out where I can give it all away. I can hear it now: So tragic, man. The dude made it big, but he just didn't care about the cash. He was so into God He didn't even buy a Corvette. Just sad. Yep, that will be me. But if in your journey with God it appears that material wealth is *not* a part of the picture, don't think you missed out. You're gonna be fine living with God, and whether you are rich, less than rich, or something in between really doesn't matter.

When it's all said and done, let's make sure we understand that God's blessings are internal first and foremost. If something happens to show up on the material scoreboard, then good for you and me — but that's a secondary blessing. With all that said, here's a prayer of depth for you: *Dear God, just let me have a barbeque pit, a flat screen, and a golf game, and I promise I'll make the rest of this work. Thank you, and Amen.* (I couldn't resist.)

AHHH...FAMILY

When Isaac was old and his eyes were so weak that he could no longer see, he called for Esau his older son and said to him, "My son."

"Here I am," he answered.

² Isaac said, "I am now an old man and don't know the day of my death. ³ Now then, get your equipment — your quiver and bow — and go out to the open country to hunt some wild game for me. ⁴ Prepare me the kind of tasty food I like and bring it to me to eat, so that I may give you my blessing before I die."

⁵ Now Rebekah was listening as Isaac spoke to his son Esau. When Esau left for the open country to hunt game and bring it back, ⁶ Rebekah said to her son Jacob, "Look, I overheard your father say to your brother Esau, ⁷ 'Bring me some game and prepare me some tasty food to eat, so that I may give you my blessing in the presence of the Lord before I die.' ⁸ Now, my son, listen carefully and do what I tell you: ⁹ Go out to the flock and bring me two choice young goats, so I can prepare some tasty food for your father, just the way he likes it. ¹⁰ Then take it to your

*father to eat, so that he may give you his blessing
before he dies."*

*[11] Jacob said to Rebekah his mother, "But my brother
Esau is a hairy man while I have smooth skin. [12] What
if my father touches me? I would appear to be tricking
him and would bring down a curse on myself rather
than a blessing."*

*[13] His mother said to him, "My son, let the curse fall
on me. Just do what I say; go and get them for me."*
(Genesis 27:1-13)

Always good, isn't it? Families are easy. Families get along — especially families that get prime time in the Bible. I mean, Biblical families are *the* shining examples of how all families should be, right? Even though we rarely measure up to all the superstar model families in scripture, I guess we'll just slog on and hope we have something to show for ourselves at the end of the ride. (And if our offspring just don't hate us by the time all this is over, then maybe we will have accomplished something.)

So let me tell you about this one family, a chosen family, to be sure. They're a family whose legacy is to produce a nation after God's own heart — one that will be in the history books forever. *That* kind of family. Let's start with mom and dad, Isaac and Rebekah, parents of destiny. For starters, regarding their kids, they played favorites. If you look at Genesis 25:27-28, it's right there. Isaac likes Esau better. Mom preferred Jacob. I don't think it was subtle or kept behind closed doors either. I think it was out in the open and understood.

So, let's visit about marriage and family for a little bit. Let me say this as delicately and sweetly as I know how for all of you beautiful people who have kids out there ... or may be thinking about it. If you think it's natural, justified, normal, or appropriate to have a favorite kid within the herd ... with all the respect I can muster — *you're an idiot.* Pure and simple. You're just an idiot. Another good word that comes to mind is moron. If you plan to royally screw up a family dynamic, a great way to initiate that program is to pick the one child you like best and show it.

Let me set the table for you: I've got four kids as mentioned. All girls. I am in the girl business. I'm a little over halfway there in getting them up and out, but we are far enough along for me to say that, in my kid rearing career, some of them were easier, some were harder, and some flip-flopped between the two. We've had everything. Some like my jokes, some don't. Some like my personality, others, well, not so much. Some would make the kinds of decisions I would make others, hardly ever. But bottom line, whatever they do, whatever they're like or not like, whatever they think or don't think, whether the DI (Drama Index) — is high or low with any of them, they know — they *know*, that dear old Dad and Mom will love 'em all *just the same*. It's all equal, baby. That's the way it is. It's not based on feelings, friendship, or DNA .... it's based on what's *right*. It makes no difference that one's more like you; processes like you, connects with you — I don't care. It doesn't matter. Even-Steven. Every time. If you're not playing favorites, don't start. And if you are doing it — knock it off. If back in the day it happened to you, then guess what? *You* are the cycle buster. The garbage rolling downhill stops with you.

But back to our "chosen" family's dysfunction. Playing favorites is one thing, but why stop there? When we look a little further, we see that Isaac and Rebekah did a good job in the lying and cheating department, too. Especially when it came to Mom and Baby Boy #2. Nothing deep to figure out here; Mom loves Jacob more, wants him to get the blessing that's normally due to the firstborn. Remember that these two boys are twins, but Esau came out first, so he wins. But Mom's a conniver, and she orchestrates a ruse to have Dad give the #1 blessing to Jacob rather than Esau, and hopefully secures his place as the number one son.

To give you the Cliffs Notes on the scheme, she gets Isaac to believe that Jacob is really Esau (Isaac is *really* old at this point; can't tell one kid from the other; so, he gets taken advantage of, bless his sweet heart), and then sure enough, he blesses Jacob with everything that *should* have gone to Esau. (It's in Genesis 27:27-29 if you want to check my story.) Now to be fair, there's a lot riding on being the main heir. Basically you get most every-thing when dear old Dad goes. Family business, most of the wealth, everybody else works for you...you own it. Hardly seems fair, but it is what it is. Not saying it's right, but it's the rule. So, a whole des-tiny is determined based on whether or not you're son #1. None of that is lost on mom, and since Jacob is the apple of her eye, she games the system, and it works in Jacob's favor. The blessing goes to him.

Let's back off this for a minute. The question is, why did she do it? What was her motivation? You'll remember earlier it was revealed that God was going to be out of the box on this one to begin with. He *told* Rebekah straight out that "the older would serve the younger"[14] So why can't she just go with it?

It's simple. Rebekah wants what all of us want. What we've been wanting ever since Adam and Eve bit the apple. It is that deep, primal desire that drives us to action, rightly or wrongly, for better or worse, and we all succumb to it. I'm talking about one thing and one thing only: *control.*

Rebekah wanted control. Pure and simple. This one is not hard to figure out. Forget the fact that God *told* her that Jacob would be the one to carry the family torch. That wasn't good enough. She's gonna help God out a little. May have even felt that the end run around Esau and Isaac was merited. I mean, that was the plan,

---

[14] Genesis 27:22-23

right? Why not move it along, seal the deal, put the stamp on it and just polish it off? Help the Almighty out a little bit? A mom's gotta do what a mom's gotta do, right? I mean, following God is great, but business is business. Sure. Makes perfect sense. So, let's just see how well this plan works out.

FRICTION

⁴¹ Esau held a grudge against Jacob because of the blessing his father had given him. He said to himself, "The days of mourning for my father are near; then I will kill my brother Jacob."

⁴² When Rebekah was told what her older son Esau had said, she sent for her younger son Jacob and said to him, "Your brother Esau is planning to avenge himself by killing you. ⁴³ Now then, my son, do what I say: Flee at once to my brother Laban in Harran. ⁴⁴ Stay with him for a while until your brother's fury subsides. ⁴⁵ When your brother is no longer angry with you and forgets what you did to him, I'll send word for you to come back from there. Why should I lose both of you in one day?"

⁴⁶ Then Rebekah said to Isaac, "I'm disgusted with living because of these Hittite women. If Jacob takes a wife from among the women of this land, from Hittite women like these, my life will not be worth living." (Genesis 27:41-46)

No surprise here. Esau's angry — and that's putting lipstick on it. He's really angry. Like, enraged, rabid angry. Angry enough the script says that the first chance he gets he's killing baby brother and will enjoy doing it. I wonder how family dinners went for them after that, much less what the holiday season was like. Let's see, a wife and mom that lies and cheats to get her way, and one brother who wants to kill the other one. Such harmony! But it doesn't matter — the deal is done, and now it's game on. So, what is there for us to learn?

Folks, the bottom line is, when God puts a plan in place, He doesn't need us to improvise. He leads, we follow ... not the other way around! Most of us have it backwards. Most of us want to lead and have God follow us to make sure it works out. You know, God rides shotgun, but we control the wheel. We call the shots and — if we need Him — we'll ask God to make it right. If we're truthful, what we want is God's participation, not His leadership. Go on, just admit it: we all want to take the reins at some point. We all want to call the shots. But as believers and followers of God, our part is to let Him take the lead, and then *whatever* His plan may be, to let that plan play out. Just let it play out. Have some patience. Have a little faith, man ... just a little bit!

I'll bet if we're honest with one another, we could all remember times of serious stress and strain in our lives where we torpedoed ourselves because of rash decisions. We didn't wait on God; we just went for it. Had to make a move, couldn't toe the line any longer, so we followed the advice of old Frank Sinatra and did it "Myyyy Waaaay." Great song, lousy advice. When you and I take God seriously, when we *really* want Him as Lord of our life, then that means we do it God's way, *not* our way. Yes, we probably wait, and maybe we wait longer. Yes, there may be pain involved. Yes, we may not see as much progress as we'd like. But trust me here — *trust me* — God knows what He's doing. Whatever the situation, *He* will have the last word, and man, that's how you and I want it to be.

So back to the script. After the hand is played and mom gets word of #1 son's plan to rip his brother to shreds, she comes up with the idea to get Jacob out of there. Specifically, she wants to send him back to her hometown. Just get him out. What she told Jacob — and herself — was that this will just be for a bit. Esau will get over all this, it'll blow over, no big deal. So let me take care of all this and we'll have him home for Christmas, don't you worry. Yeah well, let me clue you in. the holidays came and went,

Jacob didn't make it back home, and to get to the end of it, he never went back home. His dad died, Rebekah died, and she never saw her favorite son again.

Ironically, the son she juked out of his inheritance is the one that she ended up living with. You think she felt good about all this? Is that how it was supposed to shake out? I doubt it. What a complete train wreck. But here's the thing — and this is what was lost on Rebekah. God said that in the fullness of time, He would ensure that the blessing of the bloodline would go through Jacob. What she wanted for Jacob would have happened anyway. She didn't need to blow up her family to make God's plan work! He had this from the get-go.

Guess what? God's got His plan for you and me as well. I don't know all the details, don't know how long it will take, don't know the when, the where, or the how, but what I do know is that *God's got this*! We participate, we follow, we stay on track, and He's got this. The whole circus with Jacob and Esau could have been avoided if Rebekah had just stood down, stayed on point, and lived one day at a time, but no. She took matters into her own hands, and just blew it all up. You and I don't need that kind of grief, so let's take a hint from all this and learn what *not* to do, and let God lead as best we can.

THANK GOD FOR PATIENCE

Jacob left Beersheba and set out for Harran. When he reached a certain place, he stopped for the night because the sun had set. Taking one of the stones there, he put it under his head and lay down to sleep. He had a dream in which he saw a stairway resting on the earth, with its top reaching to heaven, and the angels of God were ascending and descending on it. There above it stood the LORD, and he said: "I am the LORD, the God of your father Abraham and the God of Isaac. I will give you and your descendants the land on which you are lying. Your descendants will be like the dust of the earth, and you will spread out to the west and to the east, to the north and to the south. All peoples on earth will be blessed through you and your offspring. I am with you and will watch over you wherever you go, and I will bring you back to this land. I will not leave you until I have done what I have promised you." (Genesis 28:10-15)

In the midst of all the family drama, our boy Jacob is now on his way. Maybe the more accurate description is, *God* is on His way — with Jacob in tow. Leaving kith and kin, he is heading out to his uncle's place. Note here that the baton is being passed. Isaac and Rebekah have been the focus of the script, but now it's Jacob's turn. We don't know how far away Jacob is going, but it's far enough for him to camp out a few nights on the way there. Night one, he calls it quits, sets up camp, and hits the hay (or as the passage says, finds a nice soft rock to put his head on). While dozing, he has a dream, and it's a significant one. He sees a ladder coming out of the heavens, and angels are going up and down the ladder. Then God Almighty himself appears and says to Jacob, "My plan and my promise will continue, and you're in the headlights of it all. A nation I promised to build through your grandad and dad is now on *you*. My blessing will go right through you and through all your future offspring, (Our boy is not married, mind you, but that's a minor detail) and my plan of redemption and salvation for time and eternity now rests on your shoulders. Have a good night."

Before we keep going, I've got to stop and make note of something. Can I just say that it is very refreshing and comforting to know that God has so much patience? It's a huge relief to see that even in the midst of dealing with one screwed up family — a family ripped apart by deceit, trickery, favoritism, jealousy, and anger — God doesn't throw in the towel and say, "I'm just so *done* with you people!" Nope, He just keeps working with what He has. In His sovereignty, His incredible patience, His love, His forgiveness, and His mercy, He stays with the plan and the promise moves forward.

I'll probably say it or refer to it a hundred times before we're through, but regardless, thank God that He is the way He is. Thank God! Our mess ups may not get as much press as Isaac's wonderful little family got, but you and I both know we aren't as pure as the new driven snow, either. Speaking for myself, there have been times in my little life where, if I haven't out-and-out gone off the rails, I've sure thought about it. Obsessed with money, sex, power, position, accomplishment, lust, possessions, experiences, passions, acquisitions ...you name it, I've done it, or at least wanted to. And even now, I still struggle with some of it — but yet, *but yet* ... God doesn't give up on me. He doesn't throw me back or throw me out; He stays with me in *spite* of myself. I would like to think that I'm getting better, maybe getting wiser, dare I say even growing in godly character and actually maturing (some would question it), but make no mistake, I can be as vulnerable to the royal screw up as anyone.

What's really important here is that you and I understand that God has His hand on us. There is a plan in place — His plan for us — and He will stay with it and with us, through it all. How cool. How incredibly cool! Not only is it refreshing, it's also just a freaking relief! You and I are still in the game! It may not feel that way — I get it — but it doesn't change God's intent and His desire to see us all the way through. Regarding how inadequate you may feel, take a look at our guy Jacob. Here he is, a man of destiny, all alone, a fugitive *from his own family*, going to live with an uncle who he doesn't even know. Earlier he was leading a life of affluence, but now he has no idea what's next. Truly, all he's thinking is that he's grateful to get out of the house before his brother tears him to pieces. How much vision and destiny do you think he's feeling now? How significant do you think he's feeling? Dude's just lucky to get out of the house with his head attached. Trust me, he's not thinking about his place in history or what kind of legacy he will leave — he's just hoping to get by and get safe, and then here comes the dream — this trailer of things to come, this preview, if you will.

So once again, *once again*, we see the evidence that something good is on the horizon. There's that hope, and there is that future. If you get nothing else out of this book, at least walk away with the understanding that one of the biggest — maybe *the* biggest — promises that God provides — is the promise of a future and a hope. It gets me revved up just writing about it. Further, you need to understand that this is not just for privileged people, the "right people," the "fortunate few," or any other worldly phrase you want to use. It's for *us*.

With that in mind, take heart. You feel unloved, unappreciated, underused, inefficient, unqualified, undervalued, and illequipped? You couldn't get much worse than our main character: sleeping with the scorpions while using a rock for a pillow isn't how I would describe someone at the pinnacle of success. But as you will see, God uses *all* of us, no matter where we are or how we got there and puts us on the path and in the plan — His plan. So, stand by sweetheart, God most assuredly is not done with you *or* me ... not yet. We are definitely still a part of the program.

A Lime Tree

¹⁶ When Jacob awoke from his sleep, he thought, "Surely the LORD is in this place, and I was not aware of it." ¹⁷ He was afraid and said, "How awesome is this place! This is none other than the house of God; this is the gate of heaven." ¹⁸ Early the next morning Jacob took the stone he had placed under his head and set it up as a pillar and poured oil on top of it. ¹⁹ He called that place Bethel, though the city used to be called Luz. ²⁰ Then Jacob made a vow, saying, "If God will be with me and will watch over me on this journey I am taking and will give me food to eat and clothes to wear ²¹ so that I return safely to my father's household, then the LORD will be my God ²² and this stone that I have set up as a pillar will be God's house, and of all that you give me I will give you a tenth."(Genesis 28:16-22)

Jacob has a fantastic dream, complete with angels and the promise of a nation coming through him, and to say the least, he's moved. He feels like he should do something in response to show that he appreciates the dream. So, he makes an acknowledgement, a promise. Stronger than that, really ... he makes a *vow*. Back in the day, you didn't make vows lightly. They were pretty much an irrevocable contract, and you kept that contract, even if it costs somebody their life.

Jacob is so overwhelmed by God's presence and involvement in his life that he basically says, "God, I've got blessings busting out everywhere; a huge family, great wealth, a brother that didn't kill me, a long life, a future, a hope, a plan for my life and those after me...and as a result of all you're doing for me, I feel led, I *want*, to give something back. Share the love, show I care, give you a token of my gratitude. So, to put meat on those bones God, for every 10 sheep you give to me, I give one back to you. For every 10 stalks of grain you allow me to grow, one goes back to you. For every goat, every cow, every dollar I make, whatever I get as a result of you blessing me — you get a tenth of it back."

Welcome to the tithe, ladies and gentlemen. The concept of giving back in appreciation for what The Almighty has given us. There's a lot of debate and discussion on what we're to give and how we do it. My Southern Baptist buddies will tell you that 10% of what you make is what you give, and I get that. But the point I really want to make is, when you get God in your life, you get grateful. It just happens. It's a natural response. If you're not grateful and thankful for God being in your life, we have problems. A godly life is a grateful life. And a result of being grateful is that you want to give something. Something. Anything, but *something*.

So now it's testimony time. Growing up, I was an only child. As such, I have the gift of self-centeredness. It's all about me. Furthermore, not only am I used to it, I rather like it. So, what do you like to spend money on? As for me, right now, I'm into tennis clothes. Boots and shirts that are made to wear un-tucked. Barbeque pits. Have a real cool one that just came in, and now I want one on a trailer. Still want the motorcycle, thinking about maybe buying property or just spending time somewhere a little bit cooler than the resort city of Houston in July and August — as lovely as it is at that time of year. Thought about those cool RV's, too — some of those bad boys are nicer than most homes I've been in — just tool all around the country in one of those. They even have WiFi — how practical! You see where this is going? It is all about me! Some of you, you're right there with me.

So, on a recent Saturday, I go out with a group of guys from a church to a sweet lady's house. It is a humble house, okay? See, this lady is up in years, and she's a widow. Don't know her story, don't know the history, but she's alone, and to be blunt, that may not change. So, every few Saturdays this church rounds up some guys to go to people like her and do guy things. There were six of us. There were sheetrock issues, cracks in plaster issues, door issues, garage issues ... you get it? So, we're assigned some jobs. Me and another financial guy — they put us in her yard pulling weeds. Lots of weeds to pull. Could have been at my tennis club for a doubles match, but I'm out pulling weeds. Then I got promoted. Got to get on a ladder in her garage and put up and arrange boxes. Thanksgiving boxes, Christmas boxes, Fall Festival boxes ... your boy put 'em up there. Somewhere along the line, this sweet lady says that her yard now looks so good — it's the size of a postage stamp — that she wants to put a lime tree in there, but she won't right now, because they are $50, and that's too expensive. $50. It's slightly less than the cost of an Adidas tennis shirt that I would buy to go with the 14 others I already have, and it probably will not help me play any better.

Well, this lady is getting a lime tree. Oh yeah. If I have my way with it, she'll get two. Why? I have a job. I've been blessed. I've had the opportunity to get an education. A family who loved me and looked out for me. I have clothes. I have food. I have air conditioning. I have a sense of self-worth. And I'm grateful! So, guess what? I give! Lime trees, clothes, money, furniture, time, resources, whatever, you name it, I need — and want — to give it. Give it! Give, give, give, give, and give some more!

Oh, and one more thing: Not only do I give, but I also need to like it. Feel good about it. No one needs this lesson more than me. Where does that urge to give come from? It comes from the Almighty, my friends. Whatever I haven't accomplished in this life so far, whatever I don't have should be eclipsed by what I *do* have, and the biggest thing I have in my life is God. I've been blessed with that future and that hope. I have God in my life. It's even more important that a world class swimming pool (if you can believe that), but it's true. So, I hope that as we all go forward — starting with myself — we get grateful. And as we get grateful, we start to give it back. It's good living. Great for mental health. Will make you feel better about yourself. This is tough to write, as I suffer from chronic selfishness, but still, I know that giving is a part of the bigger picture.

IT'S MESSED UP

(I know this passage is long. Humor me and go with it.)

Then Jacob continued on his journey and came to the land of the eastern peoples. There he saw a well in the open country, with three flocks of sheep lying near it because the flocks were watered from that well. The stone over the mouth of the well was large. When all the flocks were gathered there, the shepherds would roll the stone away from the well's mouth and water the sheep. Then they would return the stone to its place over the mouth of the well.

Jacob asked the shepherds, "My brothers, where are you from?"

"We're from Harran," they replied.

He said to them, "Do you know Laban, Nahor's grandson?"

"Yes, we know him," they answered.

Then Jacob asked them, "Is he well?"

"Yes, he is," they said, "and here comes his daughter Rachel with the sheep."

While he was still talking with them, Rachel came with her father's sheep, for she was a shepherd. When Jacob saw Rachel, daughter of his uncle Laban, and Laban's sheep, he went over and rolled the stone away from the mouth of the well and watered his uncle's sheep. Then Jacob kissed Rachel and began to weep aloud. He had told Rachel that he was a relative of her father and a son of Rebekah. So she ran and told her father.

After Jacob had stayed with him for a whole month, Laban said to him, "Just because you are a relative of mine, should you work for me for nothing? Tell me what your wages should be."

Now Laban had two daughters; the name of the older was Leah, and the name of the younger was Rachel. Leah had weak eyes, but Rachel had a lovely figure and was beautiful. Jacob was in love with Rachel and said, "I'll work for you seven years in return for your younger daughter Rachel."

Laban said, "It's better that I give her to you than to some other man. Stay here with me." So Jacob served seven years to get Rachel, but they seemed like only a few days to him because of his love for her.

Then Jacob said to Laban, "Give me my wife. My time is completed, and I want to make love to her."

So Laban brought together all the people of the place and gave a feast. But when evening came, he took his daughter Leah and brought her to Jacob, and Jacob made love to her. And Laban gave his servant Zilpah to his daughter as her attendant.

When morning came, there was Leah! So Jacob said to Laban, "What is this you have done to me? I served you for Rachel, didn't I? Why have you deceived me?"

Laban replied, "It is not our custom here to give the younger daughter in marriage before the older one. Finish this daughter's bridal week; then we will give you the younger one also, in return for another seven years of work." (Genesis 29:1-6, 9-12, 15-27)

Jacob is still on the journey to get away from his brother and is looking to find family and a safe haven. Sure enough, he comes up to a watering hole, connects with some friendly folks and come to find out, they work for his uncle. Better yet, a good-looking girl is involved. After looking pretty bleak for a while there, this story seems to be getting better. Verses 9-12 lead me to believe that there is mutual attraction here. (In Rachel's case, I don't think she runs home to tell Dad about this guy who just kissed her and claims to be related unless she's excited about it.)

Sure enough, our boy goes home with the gang, meets Uncle Laban, and settles in. After a month, the whole thing is just going great. So good, in fact, that Laban says Jacob ought to come on full time and asks how he'd like to be paid. Jacob quickly names his price; says room and board plus your gorgeous daughter Rachel would be just fine (it's only been a month, but things move fast over there.) So Laban, seeing that the boy is completely lovestruck, takes full advantage of the situation, and says, "No problem, Jacob. She's yours — congratulations! You'll need to stay here and work full time for me for seven years *before* you marry her, but that shouldn't be a problem." Jacob, so freaking in love with this girl, says he'll work the seven years if that's what it takes, and that's exactly what happens. Seven years come and go — seems like a week, really — and then before you know it, we have ourselves a wedding. (What's seven years among friends, anyway?)

Now this is where this story gets *really* interesting. After the wedding and the reception are done, the newly-weds are returning to the bridal tent. Then, when all the lanterns and candles are out, when Jacob goes into the master bedroom, an exchange takes place. Specifically, one daughter of Laban gets swapped out for the other one! To be clear, Jacob sends *Leah* to the Honeymoon Suite instead of Rachel, and he tells *her* to sleep with Jacob instead of her sister. *What?* And to make it more bizarre to me, our boy Jacob doesn't even catch it!

Are you kidding me?

A personal note here: I have taught on Genesis more than a few times, read countless commentaries, heard this story told, taught, and preached early and often, and up to now, no one .... I mean *no one*, has explained to me how in the world you sleep with someone and don't know it's not your future wife! (The *only* thing I can surmise is that our boy experienced a whole new level of drunk.) But *regardless*, Jacob has a romantic night with a woman he *thinks* is the love of his life only to find out it's the *older sister* of the love of his life. Worse, what's done is done. Back then, when you made love to a woman, you were consummating marriage with her — we have veered off that just a bit. But back to it, Jacob sleeps with Leah, and this deal is closed. Done. Jacob is married, just to a different woman than he bargained for. So the morning after, Jacob basically gets up, goes to Laban, and in my unauthorized translation says "What the hell?" Laban calmly says that it just wouldn't be right to marry off daughter #2 before daughter #1 — just not right! But now that the switch has been made, he invites Jacob to spend the rest of his honeymoon week with Leah, then he can marry Rachel, provided he stays put and works another seven years for that privilege. It's as simple as that. So off we go.

There's a point here. It's something that's been at work for a while, and it's continuing. You'll remember that the whole reason Jacob is even in the mix is because he is on the run from a really hacked off big brother who would love nothing better than to string Jacob up before sundown if he could. And we know the reason — Jacob and his mother hatched the plan to get Jacob favored status over Esau by deceit and trickery. So now here we are, several years later, and deception is happening again. But now, it's on the other side. Jacob gets the back end of this one. You know the message I get from this? It's pretty clear to me. At the end of the day, you and I don't get away with anything. Period. Oh, we may think we have, and the consequences can be a long time coming. But when it's all said and done — either on this side of heaven or on the other — I absolutely believe there's an irrevocable, undeniable truth at work: What goes around *will* inevitably come around. We *will* reap what we sow, and no one, *no one* is immune from it. (My beloved Uncle Russell used to say that was absolutely true — unless you were a Kennedy — but truth be told, the Kennedy's are in the same boat as everybody else.)

This little episode with Jacob and his uncle is one of many illustrations on how this works. Now, lest you think I'm all fire and brimstone, relax. There is some very good news about all this, so stay tuned. But for now, all Jacob is getting is a taste of his own cooking. I'm at a place in life where I've seen this play out in my own journey, and I've learned some things the hard way. So take it from Jacob, or take it from me and a lot of other people: Quit screwing around with God and your fellow man — because it *will* come back to bite you.

MORE FRICTION

*When the L*ORD *saw that Leah was not loved, he enabled her to conceive, but Rachel remained child- less. Leah became pregnant and gave birth to a son. She named him Reuben, for she said, "It is because the L*ORD *has seen my misery. Surely my husband will love me now."*

*She conceived again, and when she gave birth to a son she said, "Because the L*ORD *heard that I am not loved, he gave me this one too." So she named him Simeon.*

Again she conceived, and when she gave birth to a son she said, "Now at last my husband will become attached to me, because I have borne him three sons." So he was named Levi.

*She conceived again, and when she gave birth to a son she said, "This time I will praise the L*ORD*." So she named him Judah. Then she stopped having children.*

When Rachel saw that she was not bearing Jacob any children, she became jealous of her sister. So she said to Jacob, "Give me children, or I'll die!" (Genesis 29:31-30:1)

J acob had two wives. Having one spouse is rough enough... how about two? Surprise, surprise, we have issues. Spousal jealousy at work. Probably the biggest indicator of value for a woman in Old Testament times was her ability to produce kids, and in particular, boys, and lots of 'em. Sons brought home the bacon, protected the family, dealt with issues of safety and security ... you needed sons. So, Jacob's wives play the comparison game. Specifically, the two sister-wives of Jacob want to see who the better spouse is. Producing offspring is the game. Leah takes the early lead, and sure enough, she has some sons. Four to be exact. Boom, Boom, Boom, *Boom*! She's up 4-0, and the elderly aren't even seated in the stadium.

So, Rachel's upside down about now. She's not able to have kids for whatever reason, and of course in some way, it's Jacob's fault. Classic. After he reminds her that he's not God, she takes matters into her own hands and gives him her servant to sleep with. The rationale makes perfect sense: If I can't have kids, then I'll get 'em through my servant, and they'll count as wins for *moi*. (Haven't we seen this strategy before?) So sure enough, servant girl has a kiddo. Then another one. It's now 4-2, kind of. With her lead in jeopardy, Leah does the same thing. Gives Jacob *her* servant girl, says, keep going big boy, and sure enough, here we go: Servant girl #2 has two more boys, and even Leah herself gets back in the game with two more, both boys. And then to ice it, she adds a daughter.

But before we keep going with the baby race, there's a bit more drama. You will remember that Jacob wanted Rachel from day one. Getting older sister Leah wasn't part of the plan, but since he slept with her and didn't know it, he got her too. But alas, Jacob still loves Rachel more, and so now we're playing favorites with the wives.

Is this just too good? We could make a Netflix series out of this; maybe call it "The

Women of Paddam Aram" or some such. But back to the storyline, Rachel does finally conceive, has two sons, Joseph and Benjamin, and we are done. Two wives, two servant girls, 12 boys and one daughter round out this family. How great is that?

And just to add to the harmony, Jacob and Uncle Laban take turns lying, cheating, and manipulating one another when it comes to the family business. It gets so bad that Jacob needs to get out of town. He gets a sense that things won't end well for him if he stays. So, he just packs it all up — wives, servant girls, kids, sheep, goats, equipment...and gets out. Not really a choice here, if it doesn't happen, this thing could get ugly. But something needs to be said regarding the circus Jacob finds himself in. Despite the fact that this whole thing is a colossal screw up, from family to extended family, to the family business, God *still* has a plan. God will still move forward. No question, Jacob *still* has the baton. It's on him to continue God's plan of bringing a nation out of all this. A nation that God will bless and will use, and one that will get us back to where we should have been had Adam and Eve not blown it up in the garden. My question is, couldn't we get a better cast of characters to use than this? But that's just the point. God will move through this. And he will use Jacob, despite his problems. Guess what? God is bigger than your problems, bigger than my problems. He can and will move through us, no matter what the situation is.

So, you say your beginning wasn't so great? I get it. You started out on the wrong side of the street? Or better yet, started out on the right side, but left and went south? You're a victim of things outside your control or maybe you're a victim of your own home cooking? You know what? I care, but I don't care. Because in the hands of a living God, it's *never* where you start, it's always how you finish. It's not about where you came from, it's always about where you're going.

But what is important, *so* important, is that our journey is not meant to be made alone. We have a God who is with us, who wants the best for us, and who will lead us. Am I oblivious to all the wicked, bad, unfair stuff that goes on every day? No, I am not. But this I *do* know: the Living God always has a plan and a purpose for each of us. I don't care what it is. One of the most dynamic JOYFUL individuals I know of is a quadriplegic and has spent most of her life in a wheelchair living in pain. How do you do that? She sings, she writes, she paints, and she inspires people all over the world. Gives God all the props for creating a life of joy for her. Then I read a book on a guy from my hometown who got convicted for murdering his own wife, and served 25 years in the penitentiary before DNA evidence found the *real* killer. Went in while in his 30's, got out in his 50's. (What's a quarter century among friends?) But the bigger story is, the guy has joy in his life, and has a grateful attitude! The woman in the wheelchair says she *appreciates* what God does through her. *How is that possible?* When you have God on the throne of your life, that's how it happens. That's the deal.

I may have gotten off on a bit of a tangent, but you get it; God can use *all* of our frailties. Whether through bad circumstances or self-induced screw ups, He can still move the ball forward. I find that very motivating, and quite frankly it's a relief and a comfort to know this. So bottom line, whether it's prison, sickness, accidents, or just a royally screwed up family like the one we're reading about, trust me: God can and *will* work through your mess, too.

LEADERSHIP

Jacob heard that Laban's sons were saying, "Jacob has taken everything our father owned and has gained all this wealth from what belonged to our father." And Jacob noticed that Laban's attitude toward him was not what it had been.

Then the LORD said to Jacob, "Go back to the land of your fathers and to your relatives, and I will be with you."

So Jacob sent word to Rachel and Leah to come out to the fields where his flocks were. He said to them, "I see that your father's attitude toward me is not what it was before, but the God of my father has been with me. You know that I've worked for your father with all my strength, yet your father has cheated me by changing my wages ten times. However, God has not allowed him to harm me. (Genesis 31:1-7)

So here we are: Jacob and his family of two wives, 12 sons and a daughter now have to move. One small issue; where? I mean, we're in the middle of the desert here ... it's not like relocating to another suburb on the other side of town. So, what do you do? Where do you go? What's the next step? In Jacob's case, the answer lies in Genesis 31, verse 3: "Go back to the land of your fathers and to your relatives, and I will be with you."

That's huge.

There's a lot coming down the pipe, but the primary point to make is that Jacob is being led. There is a plan in place as discussed, there is a purpose that needs to be completed, and Jacob is still a part of something bigger than what he sees or knows. So, when you and I say "yes" to God, when we say "God, I want you in my life," make no mistake, God is not interested in being a *part* of your posse. To be even more blunt, He's not interested in being your co-pilot. No, the simple truth is, God is about *leading* your life and mine. He is not the dancing bear in the background, He is not your roadie, He is *the* authority. At this point I might lose you, but just stay with me. When I took God seriously and said, "I do" to making Him Lord of my life, things started to happen. I was living in Dallas at the time, and really thought that's where it would all end up. But it became evident that Dallas was not the place for me. Turns out that through a job, Houston was the place.

As discussed, I had no real reason or interest in coming south but make no mistake — I was *led* here. So, I moved, and all I can tell you is, I felt right at home. I remember calling my saintly mother a few months into it, and telling her to not be offended, but the truth was, I had never felt so home anywhere in my life. Shortly after getting to Houston, I move into an old house with a college buddy, start telling him that I've gotten turned on to God, my life is taking shape, something good is happening, something very good is happening, and in the midst of all that, he says, "You know, there's a church you might like to visit." Mind you, he'd been as pagan as I'd been — had not been going to church himself, but something (or Someone) clicked a switch in his brain, and he suggests we attend church. The next Sunday we're there, the pastor was on that day, we come back the following week, and basically, we've never stopped. That's only been 30 + years ago, and we're still doing it.

Do I think that was a coincidence? No way. God intended for me to be at that church. I didn't recognize it, but He had it all in place. I was *led* there, through a fraternity brother — God uses all kinds of people, places, and things — but regardless, that wasn't by chance either. A few years into it, I meet a really good-looking girl at that church who had started her own journey with God, and what was better, she laughed at all my jokes. You know where this is going, a marriage and four kids later, here we are.

It all felt right, things just seemed to flow, and it's like this is where I was supposed to be and what I was supposed to be doing. And the job that brought me here? That turned into the 30+ year career I've had the whole time. Fate? Hardly. Luck? Nope. My fervent belief is that this has all been part of my journey, God's plan for me, and through His leadership, I am where I'm supposed to be. To use a military term, I don't really feel I moved to Houston, I feel like I've been *stationed* in Houston. People ask me if I really like it here, and my response is, I *appreciate* it here. I say that because I know it was part of God's plan for my life that I be here. When you give your life over to the Almighty, you're going to be led. Whether I stay here the rest of my life, or I move by the first of next month, what I'm really keen on is that feeling of being led. You see, I want His leadership in my life. A lot of people, even good church going people, may not be comfortable with that. But here's my deal; I *like* being led! I absolutely believe that God can do a better job of leading me than I can. In other words, I want that leadership.

So, the lovely wife and I talk about moving. Getting really close to getting out of the full-time kid business, so now maybe we have options. Where we'd go, what we'd like to do, what kind of house we'd have — some of you are doing the same thing. But whatever looks or feels good at any given time, I can say that if I don't feel

God's in it, I don't want to do it. If God's not in front of it, if I sense it's more about my plan than His plan, then I'm not a gamer.

So now we come to the moment of truth: Where are you with all this? Do you want God in your life as a participant or as a *leader*? How you answer that question will determine and define your relationship with the Almighty. People can get really upside down and frustrated with God when they want to lead their own life and just bring God in to bless it all. With all due respect, that's not what God is interested in. If you're struggling with this, I understand, but I want you to at least *consider* wanting to *be led*. Trust me, if you let him lead, you are no less a person. (I'd make the case you become *more* of a person.) You're not weak, it's not a retreat, you didn't back down ... none of that. To follow God is not backing down, it's *stepping up*, and He's ready to step in anytime you're ready.

One Small Issue

Jacob sent messengers ahead of him to his brother Esau in the land of Seir, the country of Edom. He instructed them: "This is what you are to say to my lord Esau: 'Your servant Jacob says, I have been staying with Laban and have remained there till now. I have cattle and donkeys, sheep and goats, male and female servants. Now I am sending this message to my lord, that I may find favor in your eyes.'" When the messengers returned to Jacob, they said, "We went to your brother Esau, and now he is coming to meet you, and four hundred men are with him." (Genesis 32:3-6)

S o here we are, after the drama with the extended family and in-laws, Jacob and the entourage are heading home. Home-home. Back to where it all started. One small problem. (Maybe not so small.) A problem in the form of a big brother ... a big brother that, last we checked, was so irate at our boy that he would have happily killed him in broad daylight and thought nothing of it. To make sure you remember, the whole reason Jacob left in the first place was to get away from Esau. But now, Jacob gets the word from the Almighty that it's time to head back home. To Esau. But hey, look at the bright side, it's been 20 years. I mean, that's a lot of time for cooler heads to prevail, things to calm down, let sleeping dogs lie. And I'll bet Esau's done okay for himself —life has probably been working out fine for him. The fact that he got shafted out of his birthright and blessing by his brother and mother — so what? And besides, we read that the Lord Himself told Jacob to head home — so that *has* to mean that He's worked everything out, that it's all good, no hard feelings.

Sure.

It's all worked out so well that once Esau gets word his beloved brother plans to come home, he personally goes out to meet him ... along with 400 men.

Four hundred men. Let me explain this to you. You don't head anywhere with 400 men unless you think there's gonna be trouble. Or maybe you intend to start the trouble. You have to understand, this is not a peace delegation being sent out; there is no red carpet being rolled out here. Esau was mad enough to kill Jacob 20 years ago, and best I can tell, he's as excited about the idea now as he was then. So trust me, it's not looking good for our guy.

Ladies and gentlemen, welcome to a moment of truth. Our chosen one is in a bind. A real bind. To be blunt, he's in the cross-hairs. The kneejerk reaction we might expect is to turn this thing around now and head back to good old Uncle Laban. You know, patch it up, figure something out, strike another deal, negotiate another solution. (I don't know — does Laban have *another* really unattractive daughter that he could marry off?) Something, man — anything. But you know where this is heading. Jacob's not welcome there, either. That split was final. He's got to walk right into this one and there's no going back.

PRAY

Then Jacob prayed, "O God of my father Abraham, God of my father Isaac, LORD, you who said to me, 'Go back to your country and your relatives, and I will make you prosper,' I am unworthy of all the kindness and faithfulness you have shown your servant. I had only my staff when I crossed this Jordan, but now I have become two camps. Save me, I pray, from the hand of my brother Esau, for I am afraid he will come and attack me, and also the mothers with their children. But you have said, 'I will surely make you prosper and will make your descendants like the sand of the sea, which cannot be counted.'" (Genesis 32:9-12)

We are getting down to the bottom of the barrel with our friend Jacob. With no place to go, no place to hide, with no other play available ... he prays.

Let me say it again. He prays. He prays hard. Jacob prays like he's never prayed before. Maybe, just maybe, he prays like he actually means it. So, prayer is a whole book in and of itself, but let me tell you what genuine prayer does:

Prayer Involves God.

One more time: Prayer involves God. It's as simple as that. If you never read another book, listen to another sermon, or study it any further, prayer gets you and God in the foxhole together. No question, prayer is our way of saying we want God's involvement.

Maybe another good word is intervention. We're saying we need some help. Some input, guidance, leadership, solutions, encouragement, assistance, strength, wisdom, peace, reinforcement ... you name it, we need it. But understand that *whatever* it is that we are looking for, the first thing that we want to do is get God involved. If you and I really believe that He is responsible for all the created order as the master and maker of the universe, then He has the answers and solutions to the problems that you and I face.

So back to the script, Jacob has his back to the wall — if he goes backward, he's toast, and if he goes forward, he's worse. On the surface of it, there are no good options here. You ever felt that way? No way in, no way out, no solution possible, nothing good on the horizon? It's all dark — only shades of dark maybe — but still, it's dark on dark. There's no future, no hope, no alternative. Game over. You been there? I have, many times; and I'll bet you have too, or you've seen others in that place. That no-hope stuff is nasty man — it's the stuff suicides are made of. Nobody, *nobody* likes being in that place. So when I say Jacob's praying, you have to know he's praying loud, he's praying hard, and he's praying long. (It's amazing how passionate you get when you're up against it.) And that's where we are.

But even though he's desperate, there's something that glimmers a bit in this prayer. Something that stands out in Jacob's heartfelt cry to God. It is a statement of fact — a truth if you will — that Jacob shows some maturity, some depth. It is profound that he reviews a promise God made to his grandfather Abraham, to his dad Isaac, and then to him. Jacob says it twice. I've got to figure he's trying to remind God — but regardless, here it is: "Lord, *you* said to me, 'Go back to your country and your relatives, and I will make you prosper.'" Then again, "But *you* have said, I will surely make you prosper and will make your descendants like the sand of the sea."

145

Something big happening here — very big, hugely big. Big on big. Even though our boy is anything but good he makes the statement, he says the words, he revisits a promise that God Almighty made to him: "I will make you prosper. Your descendants will be like the sand of the sea." He says it, even though he has a hard time believing it about now.

Here's the truth that you and I *have* to get to: it's *everything* in regard to living a victorious life. Just because we don't *see* an answer doesn't mean there isn't one. Just because there's no peace and prosperity on the horizon doesn't mean there isn't any.

You and I need to understand that what we *feel* and what we *see is NOT* the end game. My experience says there is way more to the story than what we've read to date. Too many people sabotage their quality of life because they've decided that things can only get so good. That's *not* how it's supposed to work. You'll see what I mean in a minute, but just plant this idea somewhere.

Now back to the dilemma of the day. Our man Jacob is in a world of hurt. Nowhere to run, no place to hide, nobody to cut a deal with...he's just done.

THE RECKONING

He spent the night there, and from what he had with him he selected a gift for his brother Esau: two hundred female goats and twenty male goats, two hundred ewes and twenty rams, thirty female camels with their young, forty cows and ten bulls, and twenty female donkeys and ten male donkeys. He put them in the care of his servants, each herd by itself, and said to his servants, "Go ahead of me, and keep some space between the herds."

That night Jacob got up and took his two wives, his two female servants and his eleven sons and crossed the ford of the Jabbok. After he had sent them across the stream, he sent over all his possessions. So Jacob was left alone, and a man wrestled with him till daybreak. (Genesis 32:13-15, 22-24)

There's just a whole lot here folks — a *whole* lot here. As we might expect, Jacob loads the boat with gifts for his brother. The better part of 400 goats, lambs, and rams would probably get our attention too, but I'm thinking that if Esau had 400-plus men with him on this way to meet his brother and settle the score, then he's probably doing okay on things like livestock, too. So, while it's a nice gesture, it's probably not going to move the needle regarding how Esau feels about things.

Notice that it says in the story that Jacob sends over *all* his possessions, including his two wives and his kids. To be precise, he sends them across a river. There's something really final about sending something or someone across the river ... namely, once you cross that river you are on Esau's turf. And when Jacob sends his lambs, his rams, his goats, his hired help, and his whole family across the river, he is absolutely and completely *alone*. Totally, undeniably, unarguably, and irrefutably...alone.

ALL ALONE.

No one there for him. Mom's not going to come along with something. Dad's nowhere to be found. Burned your bridges with the uncle and crew. Both wives are gone — ditto the kids. Those "go to" servants that have always been there — nada. The dude doesn't even have a tent. He is just completely isolated, right in the middle of a really big desert. (Trust me when I tell you there's nothing in a desert, except more desert.)

You know, for Jacob, this might possibly be the first time in his little life that he had even been truly alone. That's significant. For some of us, that's a disaster. Can't happen. We'll sleep with the TV on. Some will pass out with a laptop on their chest, a cell phone attached to their hand. We'll make a call, drive somewhere, do something, anything, not to be alone. Sleep with the wrong guy or gal, doesn't matter, it's all better than being truly, totally alone.

Jacob's alone. He's physically, emotionally, every which way you can define it, *alone*.

But sometimes, things happen when we are alone that otherwise wouldn't happen if we were occupied, distracted, engaged, or online. And those times can be life changing. Times that, once you experience them, you are never the same. Inflection points, if you will. So, when Jacob's sent his last kid and everything else across that river, somewhere around midnight I'm guessing, he

148

gets a visit. Specifically, it's a man. At least we *think* it's a man. Some believe he may have been an angel. Others suggest that it was Jesus Himself.

I'm not going to go off on exactly who this visitor was, but what I will say is that this person or spiritual being was sent by God and was there to do business with Jacob. Something's gonna happen in this encounter, something's gonna give, and for Jacob to get to the True Truth about the whole thing is going to take some serious effort. Specifically, Jacob is going to have to want something more than he's ever wanted anything before, and for that to happen, he's going to have to make a life altering decision. He is going to have to change. And for him to change, he's going have to fight for it. Actually, the word "wrestle" is what's used in the Bible.

Not only that, but he's going to have to do it all night. From dusk to dawn. With no help. No breaks. No TV time outs and no referee. This is mano-a-mano, all night long. A college wrestling match is three rounds of seven minutes, and if needed, one over-time round. Call it around half an hour, all in. But for our boy Jacob, this one's all night. What in the world? Why is this happening? Why is this even in the book?

Because in Jacob's case, there's an awful lot he has to get out of this fight. To state the obvious, Jacob wants out of a jam. That's the surface issue. But that's not the main issue. The deeper issue, the more critical issue, is that Jacob wants out of this jam *his* way, and the reason the struggle goes on all night long is because God's not going to let him out of it until Jacob has a change. A real change. A life change. You see, all of Jacob's life, he's gotten by. Gotten what he wanted, and in many cases, gotten it by deception, lying, stealing, trickery, manipulation, and scheming. That's how he's operated. He's always been about looking out for number one, me first, save my skin. (By the way, anyone notice that he sends his wife and kids over to Esau before he goes? What a guy.) And to get to the point — *this is all the life he's ever known!* This is how it always works. Cheat or be cheated — that's the law of the land. So now, here comes an ambassador of God. An ambassador that initially has not come to bail you out, strike a deal, or save your own skin, but one who has come to get you right.

If I haven't made it clear up to now, then let me try one more time: Our boy Jacob is crooked, and now he's in a fight. A fight not with his brother Esau, but a fight with God. You see, when that agent of God came, there was possibly a solution to Jacob's circumstances, but for that solution to occur, Jacob had to change. Why all the wrestling? The all-night cage fight happened because Jacob wanted help — but he wanted it his way.

Jacob is used to having a plan, a play, a plot, something, *anything,* to get out of a jam, but none of that's gonna happen here. Those days are over, sweetheart, because now if you want the circumstances to change, *you* will change *first.* And most of us don't change without some struggle. For our sakes, I hope we're not as stubborn as our boy Jacob, but to be fair, when you start opening up to serious change, life transforming change, that usually doesn't happen in 30 minutes.

So, Jacob wrestles all night. And as he wrestles, everything comes out. All the deceit. All the trickery. All the cheating, all the lies about life and how it's supposed to be lived ...it's all coming out. Clearly, that stuff is not going to get him anywhere anymore, and it's not lost on Jacob that his game is over ... but our boy doesn't give up. To his credit, he still wants help, he still wants a blessing out of all this, so he keeps at it. Probably the first genuinely right thing this guy has ever done. He's fought all night, he's out of bullets, but give him credit, he's not gonna let this guy loose until he gets a blessing. Whatever it takes, he's going to wrestle or die, but be sure of this: he wasn't going to leave anything on that riverbank.

THE AWAKENING

When the man saw that he could not overpower him, he touched the socket of Jacob's hip so that his hip was wrenched as he wrestled with the man. Then the man said, "Let me go, for it is daybreak."

But Jacob replied, "I will not let you go unless you bless me."

The man asked him, "What is your name?"

"Jacob," he answered.

Then the man said, "Your name will no longer be Jacob, but Israel, because you have struggled with God and with humans and have overcome." (Genesis 32:25-28, 30)

Houston, we have liftoff. Transformation to be exact. This story just took a dramatic turn. To cut to the chase, Jacob has sold out. Sold out to wanting God's intervention, God's solution. It took an all-night fight to surrender his will, to give himself over, but he did it. Now Jacob is on the verge of meeting up with a very angry brother along with 400 of his closest friends. Esau is not interested in having a happy reunion or a sibling bromance ... so the challenge for Jacob is still out there. But here's the bombshell: Even though his situation didn't change, *he* changed. So much so that he is no longer called Jacob, but he is renamed Israel.

Back in the day, your name was an identifier not only of who you were, but of what you were like. In many ways, it defined you. The name Jacob has a number of meanings, but the descriptions most appropriate here are words like "supplanter, circumventer, trickster, and conniver. Bottom line, the dude is a cheater. Been one since the beginning. Had a good role model. His mother was a cheater too. So yeah, Jacob pretty much perfected the craft, but now, after this night, he's no longer going to be that guy. His whole platform of how to live life, how to think about life, how to process life...that's all about to change. From now on, Jacob will be called Israel, which at the end of the day, means "God's people," but for purposes of this story, it also means that after he struggled with God all night long, he prevailed. He hung on.

He could have quit, said this isn't worth it, and just faced the idea that his life was over. Or more likely, maybe run another scam to save his own skin, whatever. But he didn't. He just didn't. So, what we have now is a changed man. Truly, a changed man. A man that for probably the first time in his life has had an encounter with the Almighty. And whatever else happens from here on out, one thing is for sure: After this night, Jacob will never, ever be the same. He will now be identified as belonging to God. He is now with God, His identity is *in* God. Yes, he struggles. Yes, he contends. Yes, he still has difficulty. But going forward, he operates under God's leadership and not his own. He will follow God's directive and not his own.

I've now beaten this horse about ten times, but this truth cannot be lost on us. When we run up against life's opposition, as much as we want the circumstances to change, the simple fact is *we* may have to change first. Could be something with the job, the marriage, the kids, the relationship, the health, the money, the interests, the situation...man — I get it — but I have to lay it out there again: Lots of times, *we* have to change first.

Let's take marriage. I just crossed living 30 years with the same woman, so you would think I have this nailed down. That I would know most everything there is to know. Should hire myself out as a consultant — a real pro. Well, the simple fact is, there are still some things about her and about marriage that I flat out *don't get*. Some things the boy just doesn't understand. I mean, I've raised four kids with this woman, been through the trenches, had dogs, tropical fish, rabbits, vacations, sleepovers, and tutors. Had some good times and some not so good times, but it doesn't matter — there are still just some things I don't get, and so, guess what? I'm frustrated! You feeling me? I think she should change, okay? And if I let my hair down (what's left of it) and told you everything, I bet I'd have you on my side. But, *but* ...as I continue to go down my merry little path, I have come to understand that there is another story in play. And that story really doesn't have as much to do with her as it does with me. Forget about her: as I continue to go on, the Almighty has shown me that there are things out there — like how I feel about the opposite sex in general, how I view things, look at things, process things — all of that may have to change.

Turns out, I may not know as much as I thought. Turns out, I may not be the expert on marriage and relationships that I thought I was. Could it be, *could it be*, that maybe I don't know as much about life with the opposite sex as I thought? Is that even possible? I mean, I know so much. How could I possibly have missed something? Just to end this tirade: What I know is the way it's supposed to be...at least in the gospel according to Michael.

The simple fact is that I do have a lot more to learn. Things that I thought were irrefutable truths — probably started thinking them around the age of five — maybe they aren't so irrefutable. So, armed with that knowledge, my goal is to not fight as much as Jacob. At this point in my life, I don't want to be so hard wired, so stubborn, so thick, that I have to wrestle all night and get my hip thrown out of joint as a perpetual reminder of where I was and what I don't want to return to. I want to be more — dare I say it — mature, and more open to what God would have me learn, what He would have me understand, and how He wants me to live.

Jacob knew that what had gotten him to this point in his life would no longer work. Chances are, there are still parts of Jacob in you and in me that on the one hand, have worked for us up to now, but if we want to move forward in any meaningful way, we'll have surrender. We'll have to change first, and not the other people, places, or things in our lives.

REUNION

Jacob looked up and there was Esau, coming with his four hundred men; so he divided the children among Leah, Rachel, and the two female servants. He put the female servants and their children in front, Leah and her children next, and Rachel and Joseph in the rear. He himself went on ahead and bowed down to the ground seven times as he approached his brother.

But Esau ran to meet Jacob and embraced him; he threw his arms around his neck and kissed him. And they wept. (Genesis 33:1-4)

You've got to be kidding me. No way. Never would have scripted this one. But make no mistake, this is honest to goodness reconciliation my friends. What looked like confrontation and catastrophe turns out okay. Better than okay. How about a lovefest? Just unbelievable, actually. What looked like bad ended up good. Here's what you have to know in this: There is no misunderstanding here; Esau was planning to kill his brother — you can just book that. He was loaded for bear, and revenge and vengeance were on his mind. But what Esau was expecting to see wasn't what he got.

Jacob was changed. Actually, *transformed* is the better word, and because of that, it changed the dynamic with Esau. Instead of murder and mayhem, we get hugs and kisses. This, my friend, is a textbook example of the ripple effect of God. So many things can happen when God moves in a life. Things we never realized, never saw coming, never would have imagined could happen. It's one of the great adventures of living for God — you don't know what comes down the pipe, but if God's in it, good things tend to follow. No doubt, nasty things can show up in our lives, but with God involved, something good *will* come . May not be what we thought, but something good will come. He will have the last word, not our circumstances. So, where's the practical application for us? It's this: I want God in front of me in everything I do. In my work, my play, my plans, my dreams, my goals, my passions ... you name it, I want God in it, and however it goes, I think I'll be good with it.

Believe me, there are still some things that are unfulfilled, unfinished, perplexing, and disappointing for me, but no matter. If I've got the Lord in front, that's the best positioning for me in all of this. Jacob saw that play out in a major way. Instead of life ending, this encounter of Jacob's was life changing, and everybody in the story wins. What's true then, is true now. With God out in front, that same dynamic can be at work for us as well.

ORDERS

Jacob looked up and there was Esau, coming with his four hundred men; so he divided the children among Leah, Rachel and the two female servants. He put the female servants and their children in front, Leah and her children next, and Rachel and Joseph in the rear. He himself went on ahead and bowed down to the ground seven times as he approached his brother.

But Esau ran to meet Jacob and embraced him; he threw his arms around his neck and kissed him. And they wept. Then Esau looked up and saw the women and children. "Who are these with you?" he asked.

Jacob answered, "They are the children God has graciously given your servant." Genesis 33:1-5)

S o, with peace and prosperity back in hand, Jacob moves forward. Or rather, Jacob is sent forward. One quick point here; with God, you keep moving. You might think after all the stress and strain our boy's been through, he could just retire and chill, but with God there is no permanent chill. We chill along the journey, and we are always on the journey, thank God. Living for the hammock is useless and dull and whether you like it or not, we are made for the journey. Retirement is not a concept you find in the Bible.

Anyway, Jacob is told to go to Bethel. Notice God didn't *suggest* Jacob go and settle there, and Jacob didn't *decide* to go to Bethel and settle there. Just none of that. Nope, the Bible is very clear: God told Jacob to go. This is big. Really big. As I have sought to live for and with God these last 30-plus years, one of the most meaningful things that I have experienced in this whole ride is that *I am where I'm supposed to be.*

In my first life, I was a Marine. One of the things that you understand early on is that Marines serve "at the pleasure of the President," meaning you will go and do what the Marine Corps says is in the best interest of the country. You may have a bit of a say once in a while, but make no mistake, you are sent and stationed to places for someone else's benefit — not yours. That's the way it is. In a way, it takes a lot of the guess work out of life. You go where you're supposed to — period.

One of the coolest things about getting rightly related to God is that you soon start to get the sense that there is a structure to your life. I live in Houston. Trust me, Houston was never on my wish list of resort cities to live in, but no question, it feels right to be here. The church I attend...same thing. I wasn't looking for it — wasn't even going to a church — but no doubt, I was led there and it's exactly where I'm supposed to be. That could all change tomorrow, but for now this is it for me. As mentioned, I've tried to move a number of times, but the doors that needed to open never did, so here I am.

You can take this storyline one of two ways: either you can be embittered and teed off that you don't always get what you want and you're on the outside, or you decide that, at least for the moment, you're not supposed to be anywhere else. So Jacob got sent to Bethel; I got sent to Houston. Who cares, as long as God is in it? I want to be where God wants me. The exact location is secondary, it's being on the right road that matters. I have places I want to go and things I want to do, sure, but the trump card is always wanting to be where God wants me. If I'm right with that, the rest is gonna flow. When you think about it in those terms, life actually gets *easier*, not harder. I am where I am because God stationed me here, and that's good enough. The story is not the same for all of us — some may have multiple moves, may have a few different careers, may take different roads leading to different places, but after it's all said and done, if God has led and stationed you somewhere, then you're in the right place.

MAKEOVER

After Jacob returned from Paddan Aram, God appeared to him again and blessed him. God said to him, "Your name is Jacob, but you will no longer be called Jacob; your name will be Israel." So he named him Israel. (Genesis 35:9-10)

Here is the end game. The end game not only for Jacob, but for all of us. These verses say Jacob gets a name change. You'll remember that a name wasn't just a name back then, it defined and described what and who you were. The name Jacob described a trickster, a conniver — someone who has no problem cheating to win. But after encountering the Almighty through an all-night cage fight, we get a changed man ...a truly changed man. It has nothing to do with the fact that now Jacob's older and he limps; it has everything to do with how he looks at life and lives it. So much so that to keep calling this guy Jacob, well, it just doesn't fit. It's not appropriate. It's not who he is anymore. He's something different.

Really, when we get right with God, it's our *identity* that changes. I know mine did. Oh, I still have my twisted sense of humor, I still have the same personality, I still have my natural tendencies, but when my foundation changed, my identity changed, and I am now becoming the person I was meant to become. Notice I said "becoming," not "became." This is a journey, too. Nobody waves a magic wand over you and makes you something new overnight.

Some things change quickly and other things take time, but in God, we get ourselves centered, working from a position of strength —His strength. That's where you and I want to be. So back to the name change. The overall gist of it is that Jacob's gonna be the father of a great nation, and in God's blueprint you can't have a liar and con man leading the pack. So, either you get a new man, or, in this case, a *changed* one.

Let's stop right here. There's a saying that a leopard can't change its spots — meaning, you are what you are and there's no changing it. *Really*? Let me help you with that, sweetheart. In God's hands, leopards can *absolutely* change their spots. You're reading a book written by a leopard whose spots have changed. Are *still* changing, best I can tell. So, you can blow the idea of being set in your ways straight back to hell.

You say you have character issues? Our boy Jacob had *serious* character issues. It took an all-night fist fight to clear it up, but at the end of it all, we had a changed man. A different leopard. A man who finally got some freaking character! You have issue with cowardice? A propensity to cheat? Here's a good one; you have lust issues? Your sex drive run everything you do? You cut corners just for fun? You prefer lying as opposed to telling the truth? Does being immoral come easy to you? Maybe you don't particularly *like* doing it, but you *do* enjoy it ... any of that hit home? Well, guess what? In God's hands it all can go away. Not only does our not-so-great stuff get blown up, but God replaces it with what we didn't have. So, you don't have much character? God's gives you character. He builds it. He develops it. You cheat? God gives you the confidence and the guts to do things right. You're a coward? God's in the bravery business. You're immoral? God can build morality. This is serious stuff, man ... life changing stuff. It's the stuff that matters. It's the stuff that radically changes your life and in a lot of cases, the lives around you, too.

Lots of times people read the Bible, take in stories like this one, and say, "That happened to them, but it would never happen to me." Bad theology man, just real bad theology. I and many others are proof positive that life transformation can and does occur, right here and now. With God working in me, through me, and with me, I continue to be remade from the inside out. And just so you know — it never stops! There is always more to become and more to grow into, and I do find that extremely motivating. Bad character, bad morals, bad living — with God can become good character, good morals, and right living — you just book it. The more we do it, the better and better it gets. That's what on the table, so you think on that, and open yourself up to it.

THE PATH

*And God said to him, "I am God Almighty; be fruitful
and increase in number. A nation and a community of nations will come from you, and kings will be
among your descendants. The land I gave to Abraham
and Isaac I also give to you, and I will give this land
to your descendants after you." Then God went up
from him at the place where he had talked with him.
(Genesis 35:11-13)*

The upshot of all this? Now that Jacob is Israel, now that life
change has occurred, *now* God says we're ready to go. Now
we can see some of that blessing coming through. Ladies and
gentlemen, this is how it works! God moves when God is ready —
which typically means when we have been *made* ready. When I put
myself in the Petri dish for observation, I've seen time after time
that when I am centered on God — when I get rightly related to
Him — *then* I see the changes come in my circumstances. Either
circumstances change, or my feelings change, but whichever way
it goes, it works. If God's in it, I'm good with it.

You and I have to get to that place man — we have to always
be willing to let God work in us *first*. And whether the journey is
easy or hard, when we get right with God and ourselves, we find a
future and a hope. Truly, we are on a path, on our way. Jacob (now
Israel) is on his way. It's the *right* way. Man, we just want to be on
the right road, and with God leading the way, we *will be.* Nothing

else is more important. I'm preaching to myself while I'm writing this, but I want that sense that I'm doing what I need to be doing, and nothing, *nothing* else needs to compete with that. What a relief! What a benefit! Finally, *finally*, I can get some direction in my life that I can count on. It took a lot of blood, sweat, and tears for our boy Jacob to get to this place, but man, he did. And we want to get there, too.

MORE FUN

Jacob lived in the land where his father had stayed,
the land of Canaan.

This is the account of Jacob's family line.

Joseph, a young man of seventeen, was tending the
flocks with his brothers, the sons of Bilhah and the
sons of Zilpah, his father's wives, and he brought their
father a bad report about them.

Now Israel loved Joseph more than any of his other
sons, because he had been born to him in his old age;
and he made an ornate robe for him. (Genesis 37:1-3)

The story just keeps going. Our boy Jacob — now Israel — is with his family. He has boys — 12 to be exact — and in the course of raising this herd, we have a problem. Namely, a jealousy problem. It appears that Jacob picked a favorite son, Joseph, who along with his younger brother Benjamin, were the only two boys from Jacob's favorite wife Rachel. Three points: 1) Don't have favorite wives. 2) Don't have favorite kids. And 3) If you *are* a favorite kid, don't rat out your older brothers. Just trying to help you out, friend. It's really bad karma to do that. *Really* bad. Take a look at what happens next:

Now his brothers had gone to graze their father's flocks near Shechem, and Israel said to Joseph, "As you know, your brothers are grazing the flocks near Shechem. Come, I am going to send you to them."

So Joseph went after his brothers and found them near Dothan. But they saw him in the distance, and before he reached them, they plotted to kill him.

"Here comes that dreamer!" they said to each other. "Come now, let's kill him and throw him into one of these cisterns and say that a ferocious animal devoured him. Then we'll see what comes of his dreams."

Judah said to his brothers, "What will we gain if we kill our brother and cover up his blood? Come, let's sell him to the Ishmaelites and not lay our hands on him; after all, he is our brother, our own flesh and blood." His brothers agreed.

So when the Midianite merchants came by, his brothers pulled Joseph up out of the cistern and sold him for twenty shekels of silver to the Ishmaelites, who took him to Egypt.

Then they got Joseph's robe, slaughtered a goat, and dipped the robe in the blood. They took the ornate robe back to their father and said, "We found this. Examine it to see whether it is your son's robe."

He recognized it and said, "It is my son's robe! Some ferocious animal has devoured him. Joseph has surely been torn to pieces."

Meanwhile, the Midianites sold Joseph in Egypt to Potiphar, one of Pharaoh's officials, the captain of the guard.[15]

Pretty bizarre, but not all that unexpected. Not a lot of family love at this point. As stated, when you play favorites with children it never ends well. This family is no different, and, while their actions are extreme, I can't say that I'm shocked. I mean, the jealously (which quickly turned into hatred) is *so* bad that 10 of Joseph's brothers flat out wanted him gone. Anger and hatred never yield a good outcome. Are you an angry person? Get *un*-angry. Bad childhood? Got it. With God, get over it. Where you and I started is not where we finish. When they had the opportunity to do it, Joseph's brothers absolutely got rid of him. Pulled up short of killing him, but man, they got rid of him. Sold him to some slave traders who took the boy to Egypt. Joseph was probably a good kid. He had some discernment issues, was singled out by Dad as kiddo #1, probably not all that mature as a teenager. I get it, man, but to one day be the apple of your dad's eye in a well-to-do family, then the next be sold off by your siblings to people that will auction you off as a slave to the highest bidder — I'm not quite sure the punishment fits the crime. To be clear here, let's get the context right. Let's pretend that this is you or me. We come from a good home (at least in terms of our material needs being met). We are well off. Dad and Mom love us — a lot. We are the favorite boy or girl in Daddy's eyes. Everything's good — life is A-OK. Then, in one afternoon, we go from being a kid of absolute privilege to a kid of zero privilege. Family? Gone. Perks? Gone. Lifestyle? Gone. Rights? Gone.

Any of you ever imagined what it would be like if somehow, some way, a serious crime is committed ... and you take the fall?

---

[15] Genesis 37: 12-36

I have. I wake up, put on a tailored suit, drive downtown, sit in a corner office, and then men in dark suits come in, read me my rights, cuff me, put me in the back of a squad car, and before you know it, my tailor made suit is exchanged for an orange jumpsuit that is *so* not my size, and my home in the 'burbs has been down-sized to a 6x8' cell. Truly, tiny home living but without my consent.

The racquet club, my custom BBQ pit, college football tickets, fishing on the coast, running on the beach, living the prover-bial dream ... it's all gone. My days of rendering financial advice and counsel are now spent trying not to hack off guys that look like they have no interest in financial matters and don't like the fact that I have no tattoos. Can you imagine? Well, that's where we are with our boy Joseph. Granted, he wasn't perfect — as dis-cussed, he probably acted entitled and arrogant — but still, he didn't deserve *this*.

Yet once again, we are reminded of that longstanding uni-versal truth: LIFE. IS. NOT. FAIR. Just isn't. Not then and not now. It's the way it is, ma'am. If God cared or if He was real this would never happen, right? You and I know it's not true. But many cut their ties with God right here. When the injustice comes, when the unfairness hits, when the bad report is announced, when all the bad happens to all the good ...that ends it. A good friend of mine once was in a season of anguish. He'd lost a son. At one point through the sobs, I blurted out, "Brother, you know God's got this," to which he replied, "Don't tell me about God — I lost all faith in him in Vietnam!"

I get it. Wars happen. Sickness hits. Pandemics show up. Children die. Anything is fair game in this life. I'm a broken record, but you have to know, *have to know*, that there is some-thing good that can come of all of it. Watch how this plays out in Joseph's case, then see what you think.

It's Not Over

Now Joseph had been taken down to Egypt. Potiphar, an Egyptian who was one of Pharaoh's officials, the captain of the guard, bought him from the Ishmaelites who had taken him there.

The LORD was with Joseph so that he prospered, and he lived in the house of his Egyptian master. When his master saw that the LORD was with him and that the LORD gave him success in everything he did, Joseph found favor in his eyes and became his attendant. Potiphar put him in charge of his household, and he entrusted to his care everything he owned. From the time he put him in charge of his household and of all that he owned, the LORD blessed the household of the Egyptian because of Joseph. The blessing of the LORD was on everything Potiphar had, both in the house and in the field. So Potiphar left everything he had in Joseph's care; with Joseph in charge, he did not concern himself with anything except the food he ate. (Genesis 39:1-6a)

You know this kid got his life pulled out from under him. There is no question his life took an unbelievable turn, and not in a good way ... or so it seemed. But this is critical — *really critical*. You can't miss this. If we miss here, we will miss a whole lot, and frankly, we may never get it right, so here we go. One key passage rocks the world. One little half verse — the first part of verse 2 to be exact — gives us a window, a glimmer of hope for this kid. It says, "And the Lord was with Joseph —". What?

"And the Lord was with Joseph —".

Do you get this — do you get it? What you need to know is that: 1) While *really* bad stuff happens, 2) God is *in* the really bad stuff.

There it is. One of the secrets of the ages. A golden key to successful living. A difference maker. A game changer as to how you do in life, how you look at life, and quite frankly, how you look at God. If we think God isn't around when the lights go out, the unreal becomes real, and the fat slams into the fan, then we miss the mark entirely. God isn't *around* the train wreck. He's in the *middle* of it.

In the freaking middle of the circus.

Not only is He in the middle of all of it, He has a way *through* it. He has a purpose in it. Something meaningful can be learned because of it. That's the conclusion you and I must come to. You've got to get this. Too many people — *too many people* — look at God as some kind of "get out of jail free" card. They believe that with the Almighty at their side, their job will always be good, their health will be great, their spouse will be low maintenance, their kids will stay in their lanes, and they'll live long and prosper. Only low-cost challenges. Nothing too extreme. Life keeps well within the boundaries...but then when it all blows up, when it comes unhinged, then where is God? When life starts to look like a certified drug deal gone bad, we're caught off guard, thinking either something must be wrong with us, or something must be wrong with God. Let me tell you where that kind of reasoning leads:

1) God let me down

2) God can't be trusted

3) I'm not safe from disaster

4) I'm on my own

5) I live in fear

That's just more bad theology. I'm sorry — it is.

Let me tell you something. I hope that as you read this, your life is nothing but good. I hope everything works out for you. I hope your drama quotient is way below average...truly, I do. I hope that for you it's just all good.

But, *but*...if by chance the shot across the bow comes; if by chance you get blindsided; if by chance the world goes upside down ... I can promise you God is there, God is with you, God is working.

Nothing is exempt.

Have you seen suicide? God is there. A divorce? Husband went nuts? Wife went nuts? Both went nuts? God is there. Been wounded, physically, emotionally, relationally? Not you, but somebody close to you? God is in that. Your job blow up? Your money blow up? Your way of life blow up? God's there, too. I can keep going and I'm more than happy to, but at the end of the day what I know is that when it's been my turn to experience some of this wonderful stuff — God will be there, God will be with me, and God will be working.

Stay tuned, friend; it just gets better.

ARE YOU KIDDING?

The LORD was with Joseph so that he prospered, and he lived in the house of his Egyptian master. When his master saw that the LORD was with him and that the LORD gave him success in everything he did, Joseph found favor in his eyes and became his attendant. Potiphar put him in charge of his household, and he entrusted to his care everything he owned. From the time he put him in charge of his household and of all that he owned, the LORD blessed the household of the Egyptian because of Joseph. The blessing of the LORD was on everything Potiphar had, both in the house and in the field. So Potiphar left everything he had in Joseph's care; with Joseph in charge, he did not concern himself with anything except the food he ate. (Genesis 39:2b-6)

Here is an oxymoron: Joseph goes from being his dad's golden boy to a slave in a foreign land. His life does a 180 turn — yet Joseph prospered. He prospered! What? How does this happen? Based on his circumstances, Joseph's life should be miserable.

That's how it should be. But here's the thing: what *should* be isn't how it *has* to be, and this, my friend, is the difference between those who trust God, and those who don't.

So, let me ask you: What defines you? How do you view your-self? Here, let me start. I'm a businessman. As stated, I've done okay. Have not started a tech company — frankly, after emails and texting I'm lost — but still, okay. Have a wife; married , made it to 30 years. Might make 31. Some marriages may be better, others not so much, but we're still intact, so I can play the commitment card. Got kids. The four girls. Everybody doing their thing, no major drama at this point, and I think they all love me (maybe tolerate is a better word), so I'll check the box and say I'm a decent family man. Stay in decent shape — don't drink (much), don't smoke (except for cigars — they don't count), don't do meth, sniff glue, or dabble in any other dark addictions. Horrible at golf, fair to decent at tennis — I might even try CrossFit, which I've heard is the *perfect* activity to start in your 60's. Lastly, I'm a Bible teacher, do some public speaking, can sing Christmas carols pretty well, and I know how to smoke a turkey using charcoal and wood. (If you grill with gas, you cheat.) So, you've got me. That's who I am. Or is it?

Let's go another way. Let's say that, for whatever reason, the job — the career — goes south. Way south. Twilight Zone south. I go to making in a year what I'd make in a month. The kids move up, move away, stay away. I'm a parental nonentity. I'm compart-mentalized. I no longer count. I protest; wave DLM signs (Dads' Lives Matter) — but they don't care. Health, my last bastion of sanity, goes too. My athletic career is over (as if I ever had one, but still), I'm reduced to playing solitaire, and I can never win a game. The dog no longer looks me in the eye — he's too embar-rassed, he just doesn't know how to say it. So, to cut to the chase, I'm done. It's all over. Quality of life as I knew it — finished. The bucket list, the things I *wanted* to do but never got to — probably out of reach.

So now what's left?

Not much, and if I defined myself by all those things, the work, the family, the social life, the church, the money, any accomplishments, man, I'm finished. At best, I'm zombie material. Worst case, we just get the pistol and end this quick.

But yet, what I believe, what I *know*, is that if I define myself by a different way, use another standard, then there could be a different ending — another story. What if I defined myself as someone that God knew, that God cared about, and that God had a specific pathway for? Further, what if I knew that God was with me, that I was not alone, and even if that knowledge was all I had left, that I would still be okay?

There's still a reason to get up in the morning. There is still a hope. There is still a future. There can still be some joy for me out there. It's *not* all over. Oh, don't get me wrong, I'm not looking for that lose-it-all roadmap, but if any of that *did* happen, with God as the center and foundation of my life, I would be okay.

Last year, a buddy and I went to a halfway house for guys struggling with drugs and alcohol. Fixed 'em BBQ on a trailer pit and shared a good word. After the dinner and talk, a guy came up to me, shook my hand, and said he appreciated what I had to say. He told me a bit of his story; at one point he was in senior management of a sporting goods chain that you've probably heard of. Had it all. You know where this is going. I don't remember if it was drugs or booze, but whichever one it was, he did it well, and he lost ... everything. Wife, kids, house, car, dog, career. He was too poor to pay postage but here he was; found God, found rehab, and with both was putting his life back together again. Here's this 50-something year-old guy in flip flops, cargo shorts, and a Def Leppard T-shirt telling me he has more joy in his life than he's had in years. That he feels like he has a new lease on life and is on his way to ... something. Not how he — or you or I — would have written it up, but man, what an inspiration.

That's God. That's what I mean.

So back to our boy Joseph. Even with the wild ride this brother's been on,

God is with him, even in the midst of being enslaved. And what does it say? He's *prospering*. Not just surviving but prospering. He's doing well, *in slavery*.

Making it work. Moving forward. Finding some purpose. Please tell me you see this. We gotta get this, man or else we are all at risk. Something could break. Life could blow up. But with God — *with God* — we keep going. He defines us, He's with us, life is not over, and we can still be good. I know this is heavy, but it's real. This is what God can do. Don't miss this babe — don't miss this. So, keep going, anchor your identity in Christ, and it just gets better.

WITH GOD

Now Joseph was well-built and handsome, and after a while his master's wife took notice of Joseph and said, "Come to bed with me!"

But he refused. "With me in charge," he told her, "my master does not concern himself with anything in the house; everything he owns he has entrusted to my care. No one is greater in this house than I am. My master has withheld nothing from me except you, because you are his wife. How then could I do such a wicked thing and sin against God?" And though she spoke to Joseph day after day, he refused to go to bed with her or even be with her.

One day he went into the house to attend to his duties, and none of the household servants was inside. She caught him by his cloak and said, "Come to bed with me!" But he left his cloak in her hand and ran out of the house.

When she saw that he had left his cloak in her hand and had run out of the house, she called her household servants. "Look," she said to them, "this Hebrew has been brought to us to make sport of us! He came in here to sleep with me, but I screamed. When he heard me scream for help, he left his cloak beside me and ran out of the house."

She kept his cloak beside her until his master came home. Then she told him this story: "That Hebrew slave you brought us came to me to make sport of me. But as soon as I screamed for help, he left his cloak beside me and ran out of the house."

When his master heard the story his wife told him, saying, "This is how your slave treated me," he burned with anger.

Joseph's master took him and put him in prison, the place where the king's prisoners were confined. But while Joseph was there in the prison the LORD was with him; he showed him kindness and granted him favor in the eyes of the prison warden. (Genesis 39:6b-10a, 20-21)

I sn't one disaster enough? (Apparently not.) So, to make very sure we get all this right, let's walk through Joseph's' newest train wreck. The kid took a hit, a big hit. He's a slave, he's owned. But in the hands of God, he still has a reason to live. Has a life, has a track, things are moving forward. That's all good. And it appears that in the midst of all this, he's still got his health, and apparently, his looks. To be specific, *good* looks. Maybe too good. By my estimation, he's probably early 20's, takes care of himself, got it going ... you with me?

So now, we have the lovely wife. Potiphar's wife, to be exact. Head of the household. Here's her story: 1) She has privilege, 2) She has money (goes with privilege), 3) She has health and looks, 4) She's used to getting her way, and 5) She's bored.

Life's tough at the top, isn't t it?

This doesn't take much theological insight; Mrs. Potiphar would like to have a fling. What's it gonna hurt? Who's gonna know? If guys can do it, so can girls — and who knows, maybe hubby has his own girlfriends. So, everybody does it, right? She's set her eye on #1 slave in charge, Joseph, and she proceeds to let our boy know that she'd like to get to know him a little better ... no, a *lot* better. She's not real subtle about it either. This woman knows what she wants, and she usually gets it. The stage is set. Everything's going according to script. Only one small problem: Our Joseph says no. Nope, not going there.

Wow. Really? Would any of *us* do the same thing? (Don't answer that — just look straight ahead and keep your mouth shut.) Lots of guys would probably be jealous of what Joseph has in front of him, but our guy is on the up and up. He's being *incredibly* virtuous, and for several reasons, he says no. Ah, but our lovely wife is not used to being told no. She's persistent, bold, and brazen. She wants what she wants, and she wants it *now*, but the kid says it's not going to happen. She finally gets so worked up she just goes after him. Literally. The script says she grabs him, meaning to drag him to bed if she has to, but again he says no and takes off.

Rejection. That's not a word in this woman's vocabulary. I guarantee you that doesn't happen in her world. Women of privilege get what they want, you can book it, but not this time. Not with Joseph.

Lust is a dangerous thing. I could write a whole section about it, but suffice it to say, when lust gets the upper hand in our lives things don't usually end well. Lust is a really lousy master, and if you get nothing else out of this book, I'd love it if you made the decision to blast lust straight back to hell, where it came from. But for now, just know that our lady is full up with it, and she didn't get what she wanted.

So, lust turns into livid. How about rage? Fury's another good word. And then, revenge. All that makes for a really potent emotional cocktail. Mrs. Potiphar goes postal. Nobody spurns her and gets away with it! So, it's get even time — *big* time. When she grabbed him, the story says she wouldn't let go, and our boy literally runs out of his cloak, robe, or whatever to get away. Wow again. The curtain closes on our lady of the household, holding the slave's jacket, and she's just burning up.

You know where this is going, right? For revenge, she claims rape. Tells everybody who will listen, including the main man Potiphar himself, that she was attacked. What happens? Joseph, who had no business even being in this position to begin with, is now not only a slave, but an imprisoned one. Being a slave is bad enough. Being an incarcerated slave is worse. At least before he had been a prospering slave; probably got three squares a day, slept on good sheets in a cool environment, breathed clean air, etc. But now he can kiss all that goodbye.

For the love of God, how much lower can all this go? Where is any fairness in this? Where is the justice? If God is so good and so great, why did he let this happen? I mean, this poor guy gets nailed even when he did everything right! This is wrong, man — just *so* wrong.

But wait. Look. There is one little passage here that we can't miss. We have to see it — our sanity and faith in God depend on it. It says in Chapter 39 verses 20 and 21, "But while Joseph was there in prison, the Lord was with him."

Could there be a pattern here? Do you recognize it? There seems to be a red thread in here somewhere. Once again, consider those classic words, "But while Joseph was there in prison, *the Lord was with him.*"

The Lord was with him!

The Lord was with him when he was favored son in an affluent family.

The Lord was with him when his brothers sold him down the river.

The Lord was with him when he became a slave.

The Lord was with him when the lusty housewife went after him.

The Lord was with him when he was thrown into prison.

The Lord was with him.

So, when we look at life and what we want out of it, perhaps our focus should be not so much on what we get but rather on who we're with. Namely, are we with God? Do we *want* to be with God? Do we *care* to be with Him? If Joseph's story has any validity to us, we have to see that the main point is not what *happens* to him, but who is *with* him. *That's* the real story here. And that story is just not for him — that's for us as well. The fact that Joseph started out in privilege and ended up in poverty in an Egyptian prison is a secondary issue. Let's fast forward this to right now, to you and me, right here, today. Are you on top of the world right now? Good for you. Everything flowing? Outstanding, simply outstanding. Or on the other hand, are you on the outs at the moment? Nothing coming easy? You feel you're in your version of an Egyptian dungeon? Maybe like most of us, you're some-where in between. But again, my question is, is God with you? Are you taking Him seriously? Learning to put Him first in your life? Relying on Him for your self-esteem, your peace, your joy? Or do you just want better circumstances, and nothing else will bring you that peace until you get them?

Think carefully. How you answer that question will tell you a lot about where you put God, and whether He really matters to you or not. I keep pounding you with this because I want you to see that having God in your life is so much more important than anything else. We think peace and joy — which, by the way, are what all of us want, are only determined by our station in life. Well, when I read stories like this one, I am reminded that that's not the case. Peace, joy, contentment ... when we realize that God

Himself supplies these and the rest of it is just ornamental — let me tell you, you've turned a *huge* corner.

A key point here: It's easier to write about this stuff than it is to live it. Trust me, I know this all too well. Ironically, I had some challenges while writing this chapter that culminated in me battling a healthy dose of anxiety and fear. When you wake up at 3:30 a.m. and can't go back to sleep, it's never optimal, but after spending a chunk of the weekend in church, reading the Word, praying, having some good conversations with Christian friends, and getting some exercise, I battled that crap straight back to hell and felt much more at peace. Nothing got solved mind you — the difficulties that started the fire were still there — but what's important is that I had peace and joy back and was much better off.

Just so you know, I have obsessed more over my career than my relationship with God *a lot!* I've been too concerned about my health, fitness, money (or lack of it), future lifestyle — you name it, I've obsessed over it. And at the end of the day, the simple fact is that I have been more circumstance-focused than God-focused, and when I'm there too long, I get out of sorts, and life gets irritating. And that doesn't just happen when I'm on the outs, it happens when it's all good too. That's the subject of another book, but I can take you to characters in the Bible who had everything and *still* got upside down with life. So, a word to the wise: wherever this is catching you, in good times, bad times, or a mixture of both, the sooner we get our lives centered on God, the better off we'll be.

So back to our boy. His story is awful on the surface, yet unbelievably, incredibly, this is where things get really good. Again. A pattern re-emerges of God at work. Even in a freaking dungeon, God is there, He is working, and there is purpose. There is still a reason to get up, get dressed, and get after it. To be productive. Move forward. Make things happen. Even in a prison, falsely accused, Joseph keeps going. Because God is with him, good things can happen.

One item to note: When you have put yourself in God's hands, when you have asked Him to be Lord of your life, then He can provide the motivation and the drive to keep you going. I'd love to tell you what a wonderful virtuous man I am; full of character, grit, and perseverance. But to be brutally honest, I think I'm probably only average in the Mr. Wonderful department. I'm *not* all that and the proverbial bag of chips. But with God in my life — to the extent that I am able to allow it — then character, grit, virtue, perseverance, and strength tend to show up. He makes me better than I really am.

That story is for all of us, by the way. You feel that there's no way you could make this work, that you should have tossed it in long ago? Well, lemme tell you sister, with the Almighty in your life, you'll find some extra wheels you didn't know you had. Trust me on that one. There have been times in almost every area of my life where I've just said, "I'm done, it's over, this is stupid, I've had enough, there is no use pursuing *any* of this." I've said them all, but yet there *is* something — or rather, *Someone* — that says, "Let's just keep going." No guarantees, no promises, no pot of gold at the end of the rainbow, but just the urge saying, *keep going*. And why not? With God it just makes sense even when it makes absolutely no sense. I think that's what we have with our guy Joseph. God is with him, and he knows it. So, he just keeps going.

DREAMS

Some time later, the cupbearer and the baker of the king of Egypt offended their master, the king of Egypt. Pharaoh was angry with his two officials, the chief cupbearer and the chief baker, and put them in custody in the house of the captain of the guard, in the same prison where Joseph was confined. ⁴ The captain of the guard assigned them to Joseph, and he attended them.

After they had been in custody for some time, ⁵ each of the two men — the cupbearer and the baker of the king of Egypt, who were being held in prison — had a dream the same night, and each dream had a meaning of its own.

When Joseph came to them the next morning, he saw that they were dejected. So he asked Pharaoh's officials who were in custody with him in his master's house, "Why do you look so sad today?"

"We both had dreams," they answered, "but there is no one to interpret them."

Then Joseph said to them, "Do not interpretations belong to God? Tell me your dreams."

So the chief cupbearer told Joseph his dream. He said to him, "In my dream I saw a vine in front of me, and on the vine were three branches. As soon as it budded, it blossomed, and its clusters ripened into grapes. ¹¹ Pharaoh's cup was in my hand, and I took the grapes, squeezed them into Pharaoh's cup and put the cup in his hand."

"This is what it means," Joseph said to him. "The three branches are three days. Within three days Pharaoh will lift up your head and restore you to your position, and you will put Pharaoh's cup in his hand, just as you used to do when you were his cupbearer. But when all goes well with you, remember me and show me kindness; mention me to Pharaoh and get me out of this prison. I was forcibly carried off from the land of the Hebrews, and even here I have done nothing to deserve being put in a dungeon."

When the chief baker saw that Joseph had given a favorable interpretation, he said to Joseph, "I too had a dream: On my head were three baskets of bread. In the top basket were all kinds of baked goods for Pharaoh, but the birds were eating them out of the basket on my head."

"This is what it means," Joseph said. "The three baskets are three days. Within three days Pharaoh will lift off your head and impale your body on a pole. And the birds will eat away your flesh."

Now the third day was Pharaoh's birthday, and he gave a feast for all his officials. He lifted up the heads

*of the chief cupbearer and the chief baker in the pres-
ence of his officials: He restored the chief cupbearer
to his position, so that he once again put the cup into
Pharaoh's hand — but he impaled the chief baker, just
as Joseph had said to them in his interpretation.*

*The chief cupbearer, however, did not remember
Joseph; he forgot him.* (Genesis 40)

I'm hoping you'll read the chapter, but for those of you who just want the Cliffs Notes, while Joseph is in the dungeon resort, two new characters enter the stage. Specifically, some higher-end players: the Pharoah's chief chef, and his personal winetaster. Top of the line jobs, have to be really well connected to get the positions. But these two VIPs find themselves in a bad place. In prison. The exact same spot as our guy, Mr. Unlucky. So, there they are. Weeks turn into months, maybe even a year or two, but then something strange and unusual happens. At some point, both our new guys have a dream. Same time, two different dreams, but the dreams got their attention. They were no ordinary dreams; these were the kind where you remember *everything*. And they were significant enough that both men felt like they had some meaning behind them. That something big was going on. They didn't know what, but they felt the need to get to the core of what they meant.

They needed a Dream Whisperer.

Wouldn't you know it, Joseph, our guy, running the shop down there, the poster child for hard luck says, "Tell me the dreams. Let's see what you got. Lord knows we have all the time in the world down here, so start at the beginning and lay it on me." The wine guy starts. Tells Joseph what he dreamed, and after the story, Joseph goes, "That's easy. In about 72 hours you are outta here, and back at the job, full benefits, everything good, just like before."

Wow. A great read! So now the head chef is pumped. Can't wait to share *his* dream. He puts it out there, Joseph listens, and basically says, "Dude, in the same 72 hours you also are getting out, but that's not great news, because it's not back to the kitchen for you. It's straight to the chopping block, where your head will be removed from your body. It's a short script for you, chef."

Regardless, Joseph is spot on — wine guy is good, chef guy is good as dead. One lives, one dies. Joseph saw it all. And seeing the story for what it is, he makes a request to the wine guy. Before the cupbearer left, Joseph asked him to put a good word in for him with Pharaoh. You know, a little something for the effort. Can't hurt anything, and it might go a long way, you know? So of course, he agrees. But when our sommelier gets back out in the fresh air, he promptly forgets about our guy. I bet he didn't think twice. He's outta there — life is good! The Bible says it best: "He forgot him."

Let me stop here and lay out another teaching point. Sometime — no, scratch that, a lot of the time — God does not seem to be around, and if He is, He really doesn't move on our timetable. There it is again. I know it's tough truth, but it's truth. In our natural mind, Joseph has *beyond* paid his dues. There is no justification in what is happening to him. But you have got to hang with me when I say that, again, God works in His way, on His time. And at least in my little life, His timeline and my timeline just don't match up very much.

Let's talk about that for a little bit. So, we're in the middle of Joseph and his journey; I'm now comparing it to mine. Remember, I'm not a full-time teacher, preacher, writer, or wise man. I'm a business guy. I have a full-time career. Not only a career, but we're trying to build this thing. I know I've said it before, but in trying to hit the long ball on this journey, I've have always had the nagging feeling that I'm just behind. A late bloomer, immature, naïve, slow to the party, some talent in some things, not so much in others, short on vision, not real deep, missed the boat on a few things. Pick one, or just add it all up: I. AM. BEHIND. Everybody else is smarter, prettier, more successful, more put together, and got there quicker. Just call me the caboose.

It's not fair. Frustrating is not a strong enough word. But you know the thing that kills me? Let's say I finally get there, knock it all the way out of the park, just crush it ... but I'm too old to enjoy it, flaunt it, brag about it, and truly impress people I don't know and wouldn't like. Just rips me up. Nobody will care — which is just a horrible hideous thought. Yet when I read about Joseph or about Abraham the 100-year-old first time dad or even about Jacob, I realize that there is more to the story. Maybe there are other things in play here. If the Almighty wanted me to be King of the Hill, He could make it happen by 7:00 a.m. CST tomorrow. But the fact that He hasn't tells me that there are other things going on. Perhaps there are things to learn, things to experience, things to appreciate, things to understand. Maybe there's more maturity to attain, more character to build. Man — I don't know how much more character I need, but regardless, *regardless*, what I do know is that whether I make it to the big screen or not — I'm staying with God. That is what is most important — by far.

Yeah, I'm competitive, I'm driven, I want it all, you bet I do. But what I want more is to say I stayed on point with God. And when it's all over, what I want my wife, my kids, and anybody else that cares to say is that I left it all on the field for Him. That's the end game. You and I can live with ourselves if we can say that. Sometimes I feel really strong with it, other times, not so much, but *that* will define successful living for us.

So back to our story. Two more years go by, and Joseph is still in prison. At this point, does it really matter? Talk about character — the guy has to be oozing it from his pores by now, but nobody knows, nobody cares.

Not yet.

THE BREAK

When two full years had passed, Pharaoh had a dream: He was standing by the Nile, when out of the river there came up seven cows, sleek and fat, and they grazed among the reeds. After them, seven other cows, ugly and gaunt, came up out of the Nile and stood beside those on the riverbank. And the cows that were ugly and gaunt ate up the seven sleek, fat cows. Then Pharaoh woke up.

He fell asleep again and had a second dream: Seven heads of grain, healthy and good, were growing on a single stalk. After them, seven other heads of grain sprouted — thin and scorched by the east wind. The thin heads of grain swallowed up the seven healthy, full heads. Then Pharaoh woke up; it had been a dream.

In the morning, his mind was troubled, so he sent for all the magicians and wise men of Egypt. Pharaoh told them his dreams, but no one could interpret them for him. (Genesis 41:1-8)

O h no. More dreams. What is it about dreams? Back then, dreams were sometimes previews or signs of things to come. But what does that have to do with our story?

A lot. A *whole* lot.

Here's what we've got:

1) These are big time dreams by a big-time guy. Pharaoh. The king of Egypt to be exact. That's as big as it gets.

2) Our Pharaoh knows something is in those dreams ... but he doesn't have a clue what they mean. He knows what he dreamed, but he doesn't know what those dreams mean.

3) Nobody else can figure it out either. The MBA's don't know; ditto the consultants, the magicians, the house staff, the wunderkinds ... basically, the best and the brightest are *clueless*. Very frustrating.

But wait. Maybe there's some help from another source. Possibly. Remember our wonderful sommelier, the wine guy, the guy who had *his* dream figured out? Well, guess what? He has a light bulb moment, something happens, and he remembers Joseph! I mean, what's two more years in the dungeon among friends, but still, he's got enough snap to bring up the incident where a fellow inmate — a young guy that got upside down with a big shot's wife or some such — was a whale of a dream interpreter. So sure enough, they run to the prison, go to the warden, and ask him if a Hebrew slave boy that got thrown in the brig a few years ago is around. They want to know if he's dead or still breathing. (I mean, in those days I'm not thinking you got three squares a day and top-quality health care with a fitness center.) So, what about it? Is the Dream Whisperer still there?

Sure enough, they find him. Our main man. Lord knows what he must look like, but by golly, there he is. They pull him out, clean him up — maybe — and in one fell swoop, Joseph goes from the pit of hell to the White House. Just like that. Who would ever believe it? I mean, let's be serious. Joseph had no reputation, no standing, no following. It's not like he's Nelson Mandela. He's just another slave who was in the wrong place at the wrong time. But now, *now* ... he's center stage. You can't make this stuff up. Here he is, standing before Pharaoh. Face to face, eye to eye, no interpreters needed. Let's just read it:

> *Pharaoh said to Joseph, "I had a dream, and no one can interpret it. But I have heard it said of you that when you hear a dream you can interpret it." "I cannot do it," Joseph replied to Pharaoh, "but God will give Pharaoh the answer he desires."*

So, wait. Let's replay this. You've got a guy that's been shafted, ad nauseum. Life has not been kind to him. And we have the top guy in the top palace who I *guarantee* was birthed and raised in privilege, who says, "I need a favor. I need your help. The word is, you're the guy. You know how to read dreams. Nobody else around here does that. So, I got some dreams that need to be read. Can you help a brother out?"

What would you do?

My knee jerk reaction? It's leverage time. Time to make things right. Justice time, to be exact. Let's fix this train wreck. "So, Pharaoh, sir, with all due respect, I would like some assurances that if I am able to tell you what's going on, if you get what you want, then you will make it right with me. Namely, I get to leave the hell hole I call home, clean up, and get out. No more dungeon, no more slave. Further, tell me that I get my all-expenses paid ticket back home, *then* I'll give you what you want."

But look what he says. At just the moment when things might change, where this whole nightmare could be over — where perhaps there could be some hope that the tide could turn, Joseph basically says, "I can't do this, but God will."

One more time: "I can't do this, but God will."

Sweet mother of God. You had this guy on the ropes! You could have played your way to some freedom, man! What are you thinking?

You know what the deal is here? It's huge, simply huge. With all that this guy has been through...with everything that has gone so wrong ... our boy is at a place where, get this, he just doesn't care. I mean, he cares, but he doesn't care. He's had it so bad for so long he really doesn't know when or where or *if* it will get any better for him on this side of heaven. But here's what he *does* know: He knows that no matter what happens to him — good, bad, or indifferent — God is with him. And you know what?

That's good enough.

Did you get that? One more time.

That's good enough.

Let me tell you something. If you don't get anything else out of this book, you've got to get this. Do this right, then you can quit reading. Here it is: When you get to the place where what's happened in the past, what's happening now, or what may happen in the future doesn't keep you from God, you've made it.

You've simply made it. You've arrived. You're bulletproof. You, my friend, have crossed to the other side.

When you get to the place where having God with you and *in* you is all you need, you ma'am (or sir), have found life as it should be.

So, it's testimony time. Hopefully you can relate in some way, but if not, then just enjoy the story at my expense.

A few years ago, we had what's now referred to as a financial crisis. Pretty big one. Really big one — like maybe, the biggest crisis since the Great Depression. You'd have to go back to 1929 to get some comparison. But since I wasn't alive then, the one we went through was my first. Banks, brokerage firms, insurance and investment companies — all the folks that run the money

— either they've gone broke, or it looks like they're going to. What a freaking mess. (And that's the really nice way to say it.)

So, I'm with a firm that's in the middle of all that; a real poster child of everything upside down. For context, going into the meltdown, life is good. Real good. Nice house, nice neighborhood, wife that doesn't have to work, good schools, good health. My biggest concern back then was that my tennis game was not as good as it should be. Are you feeling me? But in the span of about 90 days or so, the following occurs: about a third of my net worth evaporates, my career just blows, I can't exercise (had a foot injury), I turn 50, my kids are about to start college, and I don't know where all this is going. I'm eating Advil PM tablets like they're Milk Duds to try and sleep, I don't like my life, and I have no clue what's going to happen. I remember telling myself, "The Marine Corps was worse, the Marine Corps was worse...", but the fact was, no, *this* was worse.

And I had company, a lot of it. Guys were feeling it everywhere. This is a little dark, but there were suicides in my firm and others — one guy down the street jumped off a building and I carpooled his kids to school for a while. This was *not* what I signed up for. So, this goes on for about six months — nobody knows where it's gonna end up — but then, in the middle of this debacle, something interesting happens. With absolutely no vision on where all this was going and what my life will look like, I had an epiphany. A moment of truth, if you will. An awakening. The thought occurred to me. "So what? Just so freaking *what*?" Let's just say that stock and bond markets all over the world go to zero. So what? So what if I lose it all; the career, the savings, the house, the neighborhood, the Racquet Club, the cars, the schools, the clothes, the season tickets, everything ... *so what*?

It came to this for me: If I ended up losing everything, and found myself back in the Podunk town I grew up in managing a hardware store (my friends say I would be *assistant* manager) making in a year what I once made in a month — as long as I had

God, a Bible, and a grill, life was gonna be okay. I was going to be okay. There would be peace. Calm in the storm. What I realized was that if I stayed with God, stayed with Him, then comfort would come from Him. That's where joy would take over again. Oh yeah, there would be life change, but so what? It took six months of hell to get me there, but that was the answer.

So back to Joseph. He was there. He got to that place. Pharaoh, if you want to let me out, great. You want to throw me back in the pit, okay. Made some friends down there anyway. He realized, he knew, that through all that happened to him, even though life had delivered some brutal blows, if he had God, he had everything. He knew that God Almighty was the foundation and source of his existence, and everything else was secondary. He was at *that* place. You know what I think? I don't think he blinked in front of Pharaoh. I don't think he stuttered, stammered, or flinched. He looked Mr. Big right in the eye and said, "God alone will tell you about your dream. I'm just the messenger."

That story is just not for him. For those of us who put God before everything, it's for us too. I seriously doubt any of us will go through what Joseph did, but the story is the same. When you and I can get to the place where nothing else is between us and God, then we're going to be okay. Everything else is downhill from there — that's the deal.

THE MARKET CALL

"It is just as I said to Pharaoh: God has shown Pharaoh what he is about to do. Seven years of great abundance are coming throughout the land of Egypt, but seven years of famine will follow them. Then all the abundance in Egypt will be forgotten, and the famine will ravage the land. The abundance in the land will not be remembered, because the famine that follows it will be so severe. The reason the dream was given to Pharaoh in two forms is that the matter has been firmly decided by God, and God will do it soon.

"And now let Pharaoh look for a discerning and wise man and put him in charge of the land of Egypt. Let Pharaoh appoint commissioners over the land to take a fifth of the harvest of Egypt during the seven years of abundance. They should collect all the food of these good years that are coming and store up the grain under the authority of Pharaoh, to be kept in the cities for food. This food should be held in reserve for the country, to be used during the seven years of famine that will come upon Egypt, so that the country may not be ruined by the famine." (Genesis 41:28-36)

Oh, man. So, Pharoah relays the dream, and Joseph just kills it. I mean, he nails it. Says the dream is all about the economy. Specifically, what's going to happen in Egypt over the next 14 years. To be precise, we're gonna have a really great seven years. I mean, everything will work. The true Goldilocks economy. Just perfect. If you can plant it and grow it — you're golden. Rain and good weather for everyone. Whatever you invest in is sure to go up. This is like somebody saying the US stock market will go up about 300% in the next seven years. If that happens, just bet the farm, baby.

But not only does our boy call the top, he tells Mr. Big when the party's gonna be over. After seven years of peace, prosperity, and pleasure, it's going the other way. We're coming down hard. Not only is the hit going to be big, it's going to be long ... real long. Like, seven years long. It will be the mother of all bear markets. It will take back all the gains and then some. No rain, no growth, no *nothing*. The last seven will make everybody forget about the first seven. In effect, Joseph says, "The storm is coming bro, and it's coming *soon*."

So, what's a Pharaoh to do? Oh, our boy has a solution; he has a plan. He says, "Here's what needs to happen, sir. We need to build some serious storage bins and bankroll a whole lot of produce. Save it and store it. Make bank and keep it. For the next seven years you need to do this. Then, when the famine hits the fan, when the pestilence sets in, when there's nothing but dust and ashes out there, we're loaded. We're ready. Not only will we have enough to eat, we'll also have extra to sell off to all the other poor saps around us who didn't see it coming. You do this right, and you'll own the free world, baby. You will be king of the hemisphere. And your next step is to hire the right guy to make it all happen."

A bombshell moment. The pitch of the century. The Donald can't trump this one. Pharaoh can make a fortune riding it up, then make a fortune when it all goes to hell in a handbasket. Are you believing this kid? So, where's he from again? Is he for real, or did prison life make him nuts?

And what does Pharoah do?

He buys it.

Hook, line, and sinker, he buys it. Game on. He says, "That's exactly what my dream meant! My Chief of Staff couldn't get it, ditto my magicians. And my fortune tellers were useless — what am I paying those guys for? No one could figure all this out except you. So, Joseph, or whatever your name is, you're hired. You're the man. It's on you. Your call, your plan, you run it. Here's my ring and my robe. You're in charge of Egypt. Whatever you need, you've got it. So where did you say you're living? Prison? Well, not now. You have the house on the hill, my man. Let's make this happen — I say we start tomorrow morning around 8.00 a.m. Nile-time. And by the way, how do you like your eggs cooked? Just let the new chef know."

You know, as I'm just writing this story out, I have to smile. This just doesn't get any better. You can't make this stuff up.

But that's God.

That's just God.

This whole book has been about patience, about trials, about tribulation, about injustice, about waiting, wanting, hoping, praying...about *anything* that we might have to endure in this life ... and God just delivers. He delivers! Friends, I've got to tell you — that's what I'm in it for. This is why a no-name, middle-aged, husband, girl dad, ex-Marine, and businessman bible teacher writes a book. There is an end game to all this. Our main guy Joseph — you think this is an isolated incident for him? That this kind of deliverance only happens to other people? Oh no, my friend. No, no, no. This is the story for all of us. Don't misunderstand, you and I may not be made prime minister, the star of the show, or an Oscar winner, but God absolutely has an upside for all of us. There *will* be light at the end of our tunnel. There's gonna be purpose, there's gonna be value, there's gonna be some kind of a future, and thus, there will always be a reason to get up in the morning, a reason to live and keep going, because God *will* have the last word. You never bet against God. Never.

Here's a guy who's been sold down the river by his own brothers, enslaved, treated like dirt. He spends time as one of the least, the lost, and the left behind, but God was just getting warmed up. And now this. You think this is prosperity religion? Hardly. None of us would want his life, but the greatest news is, when we stay centered, when we stay with God, He's got a plan. That's it. This is an extreme example, but it doesn't matter. I've learned — and I keep on learning — that you never limit God. My job, my goal, my passion, is to stay rightly related to Him, and He'll deliver. Don't know how, don't know when, don't know who or what may or may not be involved, but my God *will* deliver.

UNFINISHED BUSINESS

Before the years of famine came, two sons were born to Joseph by Asenath daughter of Potiphera, priest of On. Joseph named his firstborn Manasseh and said, "It is because God has made me forget all my trouble and all my father's household." The second son he named Ephraim and said, "It is because God has made me fruitful in the land of my suffering." (Genesis 41:50-52)

It's just all good now. It's rolling. Joseph got the top spot at 30. His 20's were nothing but hell, but it's a new decade now. God delivered. Life changed. He got married. The Bible says she was the daughter of a big-time priest. It was an arranged marriage, but who cares? Then he and the wife have two kids. Two boys to be exact. He names them Manasseh and Ephraim. Back then names meant something. They were descriptive. Manasseh means "God made me forget all about my past." Ephraim means, "God made me fruitful (like, *really* successful) in the land of my suffering."

Which reminds me of The United States Marine Corps (especially the suffering part). I'm around 20 years old, just living life, no direction, no goals, and for the most part, loving every second of it. A modern-day Peter Pan ... and proud of it. One fateful day, the Marine Corps recruiter was in the area. On my college campus to be exact. (Why did they let him on the premises?) He invited me to drop by and see him. Why did I go? He sat me down, asked me what I intended to do with my life. What were my plans? What was my career path? (*What* career path?)

When I shared that living off my family while working toward a degree in lifeguarding seemed logical, he offered another option: Come spend 10 weeks with us at summer camp. Marine Corps summer camp to be exact. (Truly, that's what they all call it — camp. How fun is that?) He showed me really cool brochures. Guys in shape working out in pretty forests, camping out under starlit skies, jumping out of ships right onto beautiful beaches, shooting some serious guns — says I can do this! So, I tell him to keep going, and man, it gets even more interesting! Not only do I get to do all this great stuff, but, if you can believe it, the camp's on *them*. Everything's paid for — I just show up. Not only that, but they'll also pay me to play! It's more than what I'll make as a lifeguard, and so much more exciting, he says. Are you kidding me? What's the catch? No catch, he says. Matter of fact, they may offer me a job when the 10 weeks are up — easy-peasy. This is just great. Just sign here, and we'll reserve you a spot — we can make that happen, like, right now.

I did have one question. The 10-week summer camp. Was it hard? I remember his answer like it was earlier today at lunch: "Oh, you'll work really hard, but a big strong kid like you? Ah, you'll love it! And the kicker? The girls will love it,"

We're done here. Where do I sign? This is the best day of my life! Truly, my ship has come in — let the celebration begin!

Fast forward to "camp."

Week one. Wow. A bit of a shock, but hey, this is still cool. I have no hair, I'm a little sore, not getting my usual 12 hours of sleep, but I'll get through it. And no doubt, the girls will love it!

By the end of week two, the only girl I wanted was my mother. This is no longer fun or cool, or exciting. Nobody — I mean *nobody* — is being helpful, gracious, or kind. Truth be told, it's the opposite. Drill Instructors — they are not real humans — they say and do mean things. Hurtful things. This was not in the brochure! It's been two weeks and I now am interested in one thing and one thing only: leaving. Hey, I tried it. Wasn't my cup of tea. Let's just pack this up, say goodbye, no worries. I'll find my way to the closest airport — and thanks again for the invite.

One minor point. Didn't catch it when I signed up. That wasn't really an application I signed; it was a contract. Specifically, a contract that said once I'm here, I stay. No other options. I'm not going anywhere. As it was explained to me in simple layman's terms — "The only way you leave is if you're carried out." What? Don't I get a phone call? I want my lawyer. Granted, I didn't *have* a lawyer, but still, I had my rights. Nope, no rights. The United States Marine Corps owns you, son, and as for the next eight weeks, well, we haven't even warmed up yet.

Sweet mother of God.

I am in hell. Truly, I've made a deal with the devil. I'll never make it out of here.

I'm a dead man walking. My life is over. Dear God, sweet holy precious God, *get me out of here.* I'll do everything you ask. I'll go to church. I'll become a monk. I'll join the choir. Anything, *anything* but this. I came for the fun of it, but *these people*, they're not right. They're not like, say, normal people. I'll swear, they all must have been beaten as kids. I mean, did they even have parents, or were they hatched in the wild? Whatever, this is so *not* my world. But guess what? For the next eight weeks, it *was* my world.

Welcome to the USMC.

So, in that pit of hell, I stay. I'm dying a slow death, or so it seems. But I keep going. Nothing heroic, cool, or sexy about the ride. I am *miserable* — but I just keep going. Me and all the rest of the poor sucks that signed up for this just keep going. I hate my life. I want out. I'll never sign anything again. I want my mom, your mom, anybody's mom, I don't care at this point — but I keep going. It's forced faith. You just don't quit.

Then, something starts to happen. About midway through this unholy disaster, it's bad, but somehow, dare I say, in some way, it seems *less* bad. It's like I'm getting used to bad. Bad is no longer unbearable bad ... it's like, *tolerable* bad. Then, a bit later, it becomes normal bad, then (amazingly), easier bad. Still bad, but easier bad. You know where this is going. A week or two later, it morphs into decent bad, and would you believe, decent bad became (in an almost perverted way), *good* bad. Is this a dream? Then good bad starts to become *really* good bad. Like, I've gotten to the place where this hell hole is a good hell hole. Me and the guys that are left are thriving in that good hell hole of bad.

So, camp graduation comes, and what a day! My saintly mother flies up to watch the ceremony. I'm so excited. So happy. Not only does she come, but I also can't wait to introduce her to my drill instructors! What? The very sons of Satan himself, sent here to torture innocent young men for 10 weeks of their lives, and I can't wait to introduce them to my sweet mother? I'll never forget when I walked up to my drill sergeant with mom in tow. He shook her hand and said, "Ma'am, your boy enjoyed every minute of it." (Freaking liar.) Regardless, there is a spiritual truth here. A valuable lesson learned. An epiphany if you will. Here's the nugget:

Sometimes life gets so bad, it gets good.

One more time.

Sometimes life gets so bad, it gets good.

God didn't give me an easy way out of the Marine Corps. He didn't get Joseph out of a Middle Eastern prison in record time, either. But yet, *but yet, in* that dungeon of dark, God made a man out of him. Joseph didn't appreciate it then, but in the hands of God, through that whole experience, he's brought to the place where he has so much joy and gratitude that all he sees is the good. I mean, he basically names his kids Joy and Happiness. Maybe a little bitterness might be appropriate here? A little anger? Certainly, our guy could have played the victim card somewhere in here and been fully justified, yet, none of that. Just none of it! Joseph is happy. He's joyful. He's freaking grateful he's alive!

So many people lose faith in God because he doesn't remove their pain or misery, at least not in the way they want or on their terms or timetable, but Joseph doesn't focus on that. He doesn't focus on what God hasn't done, but rather, on what God *has* done! That, my friends, is the place you and I have to get to. That is when living with God makes sense. That is where we can live the abundant life meant for those who follow the Almighty. Yep, the circumstances of life can be pretty crappy, maybe ugly, or even *really* ugly, but guess what? God is bigger than ugly. You remember that. You always remember that.

God is bigger than ugly.

So, this story is rolling now, just rolling! Joseph's stock is high, and it keeps going higher. This guy is so strong that whenever Pharaoh gets asked a question about anything of substance, he just says, "Go see Joseph — he'll take care of it." It's that easy. And sure enough, seven years into the best bull market in Egyptian history, things are rocking. Good times are great, aren't they? Economy's booming, everybody working, the Nile is flowing, desert life is just great, man. Food and wine for everyone! Los Angeles is just a cheap imitation of this show — it just doesn't get any better.

But you know where this is going. Let me give you a little business tip. Bull markets, well, they're followed by bear markets. And see, bear markets, well, they're not fun. To be honest, kind of like the morning after. As good as the good times were — this bad old bear is just as bad. Just like Dream Boy called it, the mother of all droughts comes, and it's a doozy. This thing's gonna get bad — like, really bad. Food just doesn't run low, it runs out. Everywhere. Everywhere except Egypt. Egypt, it appears, is loaded. Loaded for bear, one might say. How appropriate. Got food, got water, got it all. And you can go get some, for a price, of course. So, the word's out: you want to survive, you go to Egypt. Bring your checkbook for sure, but hey, we have a source.

HELLO AGAIN

When Jacob learned that there was grain in Egypt, he said to his sons, "Why do you just keep looking at each other?" He continued, "I have heard that there is grain in Egypt. Go down there and buy some for us, so that we may live and not die."

Then ten of Joseph's brothers went down to buy grain from Egypt. But Jacob did not send Benjamin, Joseph's brother, with the others, because he was afraid that harm might come to him. So Israel's sons were among those who went to buy grain, for there was famine in the land of Canaan also.

Now Joseph was the governor of the land, the person who sold grain to all its people. So, when Joseph's brothers arrived, they bowed down to him with their faces to the ground. As soon as Joseph saw his brothers, he recognized them, but he pretended to be a stranger and spoke harshly to them. "Where do you come from?" he asked.

"From the land of Canaan," they replied, "to buy food." (Genesis 42:1-7)

Wow.

Who would have thought it? What are the odds of this happening? A million to one? There they all are: the long-lost band of brothers, so long and lost that Jacob's boys don't even recognize their younger brother. I mean, nothing. They have no clue. But Joseph knew who *they* were. I bet he knew immediately! To be sure, he doesn't say anything, doesn't tip his hand, but man oh man, he knows *exactly* who they are.

I'm not going to do this whole story justice, but for the sake of time I'll give you the Cliffs Notes. Joseph doesn't take their money, doesn't let on that they are family, and even sends them home with some grain. However, not without some conditions. He keeps one of the brothers. Says to the rest of them, if you want any more food to get you through this whole thing, you need to bring back the youngest brother you said you have. Yep, the only other one of the 12 that came from the same mom as Joseph. The name is Benjamin. Apple of his dad's eye, the only living remembrance of his all-time favorite — our main guy Joseph. Not only is this one whale of an ask, but Joseph also wasn't too gracious about it. Basically, he told them that this was the only way for them to prove they are who they say they are, and not spies from a foreign land sent to see if Egypt could be vulnerable in some way. So, there's no lovey dovey on this deal; either bring back the baby brother or go home hungry.

It's a problem. It is not lost on the brothers that dear old dad never has gotten over the loss of Joseph. It is not lost on them that little Benjamin is the only link to Joseph that their daddy Jacob has, and that if something were to happen to Benjamin, well, it would be game over for Dad. No way, no way — Jacob — now Israel — will survive the loss of another son. But on the other hand, what choice do they have? The cupboard is bare, and there is no Door #2 or Door #3.

So sure enough, when that first batch of grain from Joseph is gone, it's time to saddle up, and go back for more. But this time, they have to bring baby brother. In the middle of all this drama, you need to know that the stress level on this pack of men is about Mach 10. This whole scenario is bringing back really bad memories of the last time they left a brother to fate. They are coming face to face with what they did — what was it, 20 years ago by now? It was all fresh again: We made a huge mistake in selling our other brother out as a slave and telling everyone he died in a lion attack. And now, *and now*, what comes around goes around. And there's no wiggle room on any of this — it is what it is, and what it is, is payback.

One little teaching point here; probably a topic for another book, but I'll give you the trailer for now. What these boys are learning the hard way is that, when it's all said and done and everybody's gone home, when the last chapter is written and it's over for all our little lives — as discussed before, we ultimately *never* get away with anything. Truly, whether on this side of heaven or the other side, you can just book it: we will *never* have pushed something under God's rug. The sooner we quit trying, the better off we'll be. So now these poor sucks who thought they'd pushed Joseph under the rug have to go back home, grab brother Benjamin — and see if they can make it all work this time.

Surprise!

Then Joseph could no longer control himself before all his attendants, and he cried out, "Have everyone leave my presence!" So there was no one with Joseph when he made himself known to his brothers. And he wept so loudly that the Egyptians heard him, and Pharaoh's household heard about it.

Joseph said to his brothers, "I am Joseph! Is my father still living?" But his brothers were not able to answer him, because they were terrified at his presence.

Then Joseph said to his brothers, "Come close to me." When they had done so, he said, "I am your brother Joseph, the one you sold into Egypt! And now, do not be distressed and do not be angry with yourselves for selling me here, because it was to save lives that God sent me ahead of you. For two years now there has been famine in the land, and for the next five years there will be no plowing and reaping. But God sent me ahead of you to preserve for you a remnant on earth and to save your lives by a great deliverance.

"So then, it was not you who sent me here, but God. He made me father to Pharaoh, lord of his entire household and ruler of all Egypt. (Genesis 45:1-8)

There was plenty of drama in all this, but finally, *finally*, we have the unveiling. The Reunion. Actually, the *revealing* might be more appropriate. When Joseph can't take it for another minute, he spills the beans. It's me, he tells them — it's me! That hot shot brother of yours that you sold down the river. Hello, family, and Merry Christmas! I didn't do too bad for myself — did I? But at just the time when the payback couldn't be any sweeter — I mean, why don't I sell all of *you* as slaves at a bulk rate — just when our boy has this herd of jackals in the palm of his well-manicured hands, what does he do?

He says, "It's just so freaking great to see you!"

What?

"I am so glad you're here!"

Are we reading the right script? What in the world? By all accounts, we need to be reading something about each one of these bad boys getting their toenails pulled out one by one and then thrown out of Egypt with no camels to ride home on. But *this*?

It's a homecoming. Truly, Christmas in July. But it just doesn't compute. It's so ... backward, so, so, unconventional — like, just irrational! Who does this?

Let me tell you what this is about, folks.

This is about healing. This is about coming clean. This about clearing the slate. This is about God. *God.*

In over 30 years of living life as a Bible-believing, praise the Lord, and pass the plate Christian, one of the fundamental truths I have learned — and I continue to learn — is that in God's economy there are no grudges. Just no grudges, man. Nobody's in the revenge business when it comes to Kingdom living. Not here. Payback is not a part of the equation. Nada. Vengeance is not our role Jefe'. It just isn't.

I know that some of you, right now, want to toss this one back. You think I've crossed the line and gone too far. That I don't know what you've been through, don't know the half of it, maybe don't know a tenth of it! You would say "Dude, you don't know what I've had done to me. You have no idea the stuff I've been handed. So, who are you to tell me that I don't deserve some serious retaliation before this is all over? Sorry, but you're way off homie, just way off. "

Let me offer a couple of things here. First of all, I've been around the block too. I've had some good stuff and some not good stuff come my way. Some of that I deserved, some of it I didn't, but the bottom line is, whatever I'm holding onto, whatever or whoever I really resent and can't get over, whatever I'm nursing in the dark place nobody sees, you need to understand this: If I don't let go of it, it will never let go of me. Whatever I'm harboring, whatever grudge I'm nursing, whatever is under my skin ... it will just friggin' chew me up. It will taint my life and screw me up. Some of you know this to be true; you've already seen unforgiveness live and at work. It's no way to live sweetheart, and you deserve better.

With all that in mind, here's a pearl for you. A nugget. A valuable truth.

With God, *with God* — whatever your IT is, He can make it right. One more time girls and boys — WITH God, He can make it right. Regarding our family reunion back in Egypt, it's not that the brothers got off easy or didn't get what they deserved or got away with everything. Oh, no. You know who really wins in this scene, and it's Joseph!

It's Joseph because nothing owns him, my friend ... *nothing.* Not the lusty wife who framed him, not the cupbearer in prison that forgot him, not Pharoah who was over him, or even his brothers who sold him. Oh no, baby. In God's plan and in God's world, Joseph is clean. Just clean. No grudges, no hate, no revenge, no bitterness, no rage, no victims, no baggage! He's good, he's right, and because of all that he's got joy! Real joy! Sold 24-carat joy. Not fake joy, shallow joy, temporary joy, or superficial joy, but real, deep joy.

Let me tell you where this is going, friends. Real joy, real peace, real contentment in God's hands. That is the end game. That is what is on the table. Are you messed up about the past? You got some nasty mess that's been simmering inside you for, I don't know — forever? Four words for you: Give it to God.

Lay it all out there. Every bit of it. Whatever it is, I don't care. Give it up. Joseph did, and he's clean. At this point in his life, he utters one of the greatest statements God ever put in anyone's mouth. It's in the last chapter of the book of Genesis, and it could sum up not only Genesis, but the whole message of the Bible itself. It's the secret to how Joseph could love a pack of jealous, murderous, cruel hearted, siblings, and what was true in his day is true for us. While in front of all his brothers, he dropped this line on them:

"But as for you, you meant evil against me; but God meant it for good..."

Oh man, if the rest of this book was a joke and you didn't get a single take-away, this is the home run shot.

> *"But as for you, you meant evil against me: but God meant it for good ..." (Genesis 50:20)*

Single best statement for mental health there is. When you and I can look at everything that has gone on in our lives, especially the stuff that's bad, difficult, unfair, and just not right — and then *know* that whatever that crap is, God can make something good out of it, you and I have arrived. We are in sync with Him. We can have real peace. We can own it. Nothing or no one can hold sway over us. We stand tall, we stand right, and we have the Almighty behind us. That's the end game. Whether it's abuse, rape, murder, drugs, money, health, depression, estrangement, relationships, jobs, lifestyle, whatever ... *whatever* it is......let Him have it. Let Him use it! Use it to make you right. Use it to make you whole. In His supernatural way, use it to make you better.

Life's too short. We have way too many people that are upside down with grief, anger, rage, hurt, and hate. It really comes down to two things my friend. Either you let God deal with your pain, or your pain will deal with you ... it's not much harder than that.

It's your call.

Give it up. Give it all to God. You may not be made Prime Minister of Egypt, but you'll get right. You'll move forward. You'll have a future, and you'll have a hope.

That's all I got. Hope you got something out of it.

CPSIA information can be obtained
at www.ICGtesting.com
Printed in the USA
LVHW040325030723
751400LV00004B/70